Herefordshire Churches through Victorian Eyes

Sir Stephen Glynne's Church Notes for Herefordshire

with water-colours by Charles F. Walker

In memory of David Annett
1917 – 2004
Headmaster of The King's School, Worcester
1959 – 1979

Herefordshire Churches through Victorian Eyes

Sir Stephen Glynne's Church Notes for
Herefordshire

with water-colours by Charles F. Walker

Edited by John Leonard

Logaston Press

LOGASTON PRESS
Little Logaston Woonton Almeley
Herefordshire HR3 6QH
logastonpress.co.uk

First published by Logaston Press 2006

ISBN 1 904396 59 3
(978 1 904396 59 8)

Set in Garamond by Logaston Press
and printed in Great Britain by
Bell & Bain Ltd., Glasgow

Contents

Acknowledgments

Sir Stephen Glynne's Herefordshire notes are published by kind permission of Charles Gladstone Esq. The notebooks are in St. Deiniol's Library, Hawarden, and I thank Mr. Paul Mason, County Archivist, and the staff of the Flintshire Record Office for giving much help and guidance. Charles Walker's watercolours are in Hereford City Library, and I am very grateful to Mr. Robin Hill for permission to reproduce the paintings, and to Ron Shoesmith for the colour photography. David Cox edited Glynne's Church Notes for Shropshire a few years ago, and I am indebted to him for permission to quote some of his research on Glynne; he also helped me greatly in deciphering some of Sir Stephen's more difficult writings. I am most grateful to Christopher Train, CB, for reading the manuscript and making many valuable suggestions. I also thank Dr. Lawrence Butler and David Lloyd for their help in furthering enquiries about Charles Walker. As always, I am most appreciative of the wise and knowledgeable guidance of Andy Johnson of Logaston Press. Lastly, I gratefully acknowledge the generous financial support given by the Marc Fitch Fund, Chipping Norton, Oxfordshire.

Preface

Sir Stephen Glynne's notes on Herefordshire churches were transcribed during the preparation for *Churches of Herefordshire and Their Treasures,* published in 2000 by Logaston Press. It was the idea of David Annett to publish these notes accompanied by reproductions of Charles Walker's watercolours of Herefordshire churches stored in Hereford City Library.

David Annett (1917–2004) was Headmaster of the King's School, Worcester from 1959–79, having previously been Head of the Classical Department at Oundle School from 1939–53 and Headmaster of Marling School, Stroud from 1953–59. From 1941–45, he was a captain with the 27th Field Regiment of the Royal Artillery in India and Burma. He was a stalwart supporter and membership secretary of the Herefordshire Historic Churches Trust, and a fount of knowledge about Herefordshire churches. He wrote about church dedications in Herefordshire (*Saints in Herefordshire,* 1999), and an account of the churches of the Bromyard deanery published by the Bromyard Historical Society. The present book is published in his memory, and royalties will be donated to the Herefordshire Historic Churches Trust.

Introduction

Sir Stephen Glynne

Sir Stephen Glynne (1807-74), of Hawarden, Flintshire, was the original 'church-crawler'. He was born on 22 September 1807, the eldest son of Sir Stephen Glynne, eighth baronet, and Mary, his wife, second daughter of Richard, Lord Braybrooke, of Audley End, Essex (Veysey, 1981). His father died from tuberculosis at the age of 35 in 1815, and Stephen became the ninth baronet. He developed from an early age a deep interest in medieval church architecture: he visited two churches in Herefordshire, Brampton Bryan and Bromyard, in 1824 when he was only 17 – and during his lifetime he visited over 5,000 churches in the British Isles. His hand-written descriptions of these are preserved in 106 notebooks which are now in St. Deiniol's Library at Hawarden.

Glynne was educated at Eton and Christ Church, Oxford, where he encountered his future brother-in-law, W.E. Gladstone, the famous Liberal Prime Minister and statesman, who was to him 'somewhere between an acquaintance and a friend' (Jenkins, 1995). He was a shy man, who never married. It was expected of him that he should enter Parliament, and he duly became MP for Flintshire in 1832. The rough-and-tumble of political life was, however, scarcely to his taste, and he was probably relieved when he lost the seat in 1841; the decision was reversed after an enquiry, but Glynne did not stand in 1847 following his appointment as Lord Lieutenant of the county in 1845. Nor was he a man of business: though originally possessed of ample means, by 1847 he was reduced almost to financial ruin by ill-judged investments, and his estate was rescued only by the strenuous efforts of Gladstone. Gladstone had married Glynne's sister Catherine in 1839, and after the financial crisis of 1847, Gladstone and Catherine lived with Stephen at Hawarden for the rest of Glynne's life. When Glynne died, the baronetcy became extinct; Sir Stephen's brother had already died and the Hawarden estate was divided between his two sisters and to keep the estate intact Gladstone bought them out. Sir Charles Gladstone, 7th baronet, a direct descendant of Sir John Gladstone, W.E. Gladstone's father, still lives in Hawarden Castle. But the inn in the village of Hawarden is the Glynne Arms.

Stephen Glynne apparently had a phenomenal memory: 'it was said that he could remember the details of all' the 5,000 churches which he had seen (Cox 1997, p.vii). He was never interested in publishing his notes, but those relating to several counties have been published, including Kent (1877), and Lancashire (1893); in recent years, the notes for Surrey, Somerset, Bedfordshire, Wiltshire, and Shropshire

(Cox, 1997) have appeared. Dr. Lawrence Butler has recently compiled a study of Glynne's notes for Yorkshire, and publication is awaited. During Glynne's lifetime, he visited Herefordshire at least 30 times, and made notes of 138 churches seen between 1824 and 1874. As in Shropshire, his favourite times of year for church recording were April to June, and again in August to October. His earliest visit in any year was 30 March (1846) and the latest 17 November (1854). He usually visited the county for short tours of a few days, staying with friends or at inns. The largest number of churches that he saw in a single tour was 18, between August 12th and 17th, 1867 (he was clearly not interested in grouse-shooting!), and the largest number in a single day was six, on three occasions, in 1856, 1861 and 1867. The years of his visits, and the number of churches recorded, are as follows: before 1840 9; 1842 4; 1843 2; 1845 1; 1846 15; 1847 1; 1849 6; 1850 2; 1851 3; 1852 2; 1854 6; 1855 3; 1856 11; 1857 3; 1860 3; 1861 8; 1862 1; 1864 7; 1865 4; 1867 18; 1868 1; 1869 6; 1870 7; 1872 4; 1873 9; 1874 2.

His last visit was to Eye on 21 May, 1874, and he died suddenly on 17 June in the same year.

During Glynne's lifetime, English attitudes to church architecture changed fundamentally. The building of parish churches in the Gothic style had virtually ceased at the Reformation, but in the 17th century a number of churches were built in a 'debased' form of Perpendicular. From the time of Inigo Jones and Sir Christopher Wren Classical styles prevailed. At the beginning of the 19th century, Classical forms still held sway, but there were clear signs of impending change. From about 1750, some influential men such as Horace Walpole were becoming dissatisfied with Classical forms and were beginning to regard medieval architecture with greater enthusiasm than their contemporaries. Walpole (1717–1797) bought a former coachman's cottage near Twickenham and gradually converted it into the stuccoed and battlemented Strawberry Hill. This building started a fashion for Gothic amongst some aristocrats, who delighted in building sham castles, follies and sometimes more substantial edifices. A handful of churches in the 18th century were built in a picturesque version of the style, one of the earliest being Shobdon in Herefordshire (1752–56), a church not visited by Glynne. In the early 19th century more serious study of Gothic building was being undertaken, notably by Thomas Rickman, who in 1817 published his *Attempt to discriminate the Styles of English Architecture,* and henceforth the styles were described as Norman (or Romanesque) and the three styles of Gothic: Early English, Decorated and Perpendicular. And under the influence of Augustus Pugin a revolution in taste was rapidly accomplished. Pugin early developed a passion for Gothic architecture, and disliked Classical forms which were not felt to be in accordance with the gospel. In 1833 John Keble preached a sermon on National Apostasy, and launched with Pusey, Newman and others the Oxford Movement, intent on reviving Anglican worship by a greater insistence on correct liturgical and sacramental observance. At Cambridge, a group of undergraduates formed the Cambridge Camden Society, dedicated to the reform of church architecture and ritual. In 1841 they started to publish the monthly magazine, *The Ecclesiologist*, which lasted until 1868 and which achieved a dominating influence over the design of churches. The aim was so to influence every detail of the building that it could express High-Church ritual, which was held to be essential to the gospel. The years of Queen Victoria's reign witnessed an explosion of church building unparalleled since the 12th century. In addition, the state of many medieval churches was deplorable, and a vast number of churches were 'restored' for better, or sometimes, for worse.

This is the background to Sir Stephen Glynne's forays into parish churches. He was a man of his time: he loved medieval churches, and, like the ecclesiologists, disliked the Classical styles of the 17th and 18th century; and he could be scathing about modern (i.e. 19th century) work. Yet where he felt that restoration or new building had been done in accordance with High-Church principles, he is generous in his acclaim (e.g. Monkland).

Sir Stephen's first visit to Herefordshire appears to have been in 1824, and from then until about 1850 he frequently (and often justly) deplored the state of parish churches, especially if they were cluttered with eighteenth-century galleries and box-pews. After about 1850 he is less dissatisfied, and often waxes lyrically about some of the restorations. The notes here are in chronological order, so far as this can be ascertained; and the reader will be able to detect the gradual change in emphasis over the years. At first he used the Rickman classification to describe the successive styles of Gothic building (Early English, Decorated and Perpendicular), but between 1845 and 1851 under the influence of the ecclesiologists these terms are replaced by the unlovely First Pointed, Middle Pointed and Third Pointed respectively. He must have felt dissatisfied with these, for in 1852 he restored the Rickman terms and continued to use these for the rest of his life.

I am indebted to David Cox for help in editing these notes; and in general I have followed the same method that Cox used in editing the Shropshire notes. Thus square brackets are used to enclose matter not present in the manuscripts, and to give the volume and folio numbers, e.g. [89.11]; my own additions are in italics. Sometimes I have added in italics at the end of Glynne's description comments about notable changes which have occurred since Glynne's visit. Glynne often later added to his original description on pages facing the original text (i.e. on the verso of the preceding leaf); these are enclosed here in angle brackets. Glynne's spelling is preserved: thus pues (for pews) and panneling (panelling) were common variants in the 19th century; and there are minor variations in the spelling of several place-names. Glynne's abbreviations are inconsistent (thus Perp. or Perpr. for Perpendicular) and they have been extended. Likewise, compass points (N, NE etc.) have been written here in full (north, north-east).

The entries for Herefordshire churches are in Volumes 89 (24 churches), 90 (34), 96 (32) and 97 (46). In addition, there are single entries in volumes 93 (Acton Beauchamp) and 95 (Mathon), both of which in Glynne's time were in Worcestershire. I have also included Ludford here; although now in Shropshire, it was in Herefordshire at the time of Glynne's visit. David Cox (1997, pp.xiii–xviii) has deduced that the books 'were not compiled in the field but copied in later life from an accumulation of draft descriptions'. He provides a full description of the notebooks, which need not be repeated here. He concludes that though the descriptions were often copied long after the original visits, they do represent Glynne's original observations, any afterthoughts normally being entered separately on the opposite page, as noted above. Butler believes that although this is generally true for the earlier visits (before 1840), in later years his method of note-taking was so methodical and systematised that he wrote them at the church or in the same evening (personal communication).

Glynne's notes are valuable today in several different ways. They provide a good description of the churches at the times of his visit, and he often describes features (or, indeed, churches) which have now vanished or been superseded. Thus in Herefordshire he describes the former churches at Yazor, Wistaston, Brobury and Wacton; he mentions the rood-lofts at Kenderchurch and Eardisley, and the Norman tympana at Moccas. Sometimes he has insights of brilliance, as when he recognised that the tympanum at Fownhope represented the Holy Trinity and not the Virgin and Child anticipating by more than one hundred years the analysis of Boase. He accorded generous recognition to the work of what is now recognised as the school of Herefordshire Romanesque sculpture, praising the fonts at Eardisley and Castle Frome and the sculpture at Kilpeck and Rowlstone. On the other hand, his omissions can be disconcerting: why, for example, does he not mention the tympanum at Stretton Sugwas or the screen at Llandinabo? All in all, there is much in these notes to provoke thought and admiration to lovers of England's parish churches.

Charles F. Walker

Hereford City Library possesses two albums containing original water-colours, early photographs, architects' drawings and newspaper cuttings related to the parish churches of the diocese of Hereford in the 19th century., consisting at that time of the whole county of Hereford, the southern half of Shropshire, and a few from the fringes of neighbouring counties – Monmouthshire, Radnorshire, Montgomeryshire, Worcestershire and even one from Staffordshire. This collection was compiled by Henry Child Beddoe, solicitor and twice mayor for the city of Hereford, and in 1912 was mounted in these large albums by his daughter. Miss Marion Beddoe. There are paintings of almost every parish church in the diocese; by far the greatest number are by an unknown artist, C.F. Walker. A few were painted later in the 19th century by W. Gill, and there are also a few by Miss Goode, by Miss Beddoe herself, and other painters.

In this book are reproduced over 100 paintings by Walker of Herefordshire churches visited by Glynne. The paintings were executed in 1849–51; thus the paintings and Glynne's notes are often roughly contemporaneous.

Little is known about the artist. I believe him to be Charles Forde Walker, who was born in Greenwich, Kent, in 1808. In the 1851 census he is recorded as living at Bell Lane, Ludlow, and his occupation was described as 'artist'. He presumably made his living in this way, for he was supporting a wife and six children. He died in June 1857, still living in Ludlow. His widow, left with a large young family, lived at various addresses in Ludlow at least until the 1881 census, and worked as a stay- and corset-maker. Apart from this collection, I have been unable to find any other record of his artistic activities.

How were these paintings acquired by Henry Beddoe? It seems unlikely that such a large collection ever came on the market; I think it is probable that they were painted on commission from a local gentleman or ecclesiastic. Beddoe was a solicitor for many years in Hereford, and doubtless had a wide acquaintance with county gentry. Even more significantly, he was registrar to the diocese of Hereford and secretary to the Bishop of Hereford; he thus had close ecclesiastical connections. Dr. Lawrence Butler suggested that the paintings may have been commissioned by an incoming bishop to help him familiarise himself with his diocese; he reports that this indeed happened when Dr. Longley, the first bishop at Ripon, arrived in his new diocese in 1836 (personal communication). It is therefore intriguing to find that Renn Dickson Hampden was consecrated Bishop of Hereford in 1848, the year before the paintings begin. No diocesan records survive, however, to confirm the suspicion that the paintings were commissioned by the new bishop. The paintings must have been executed at great speed – merely to have visited about 400 churches in three years before the advent of the railway denotes frenetic activity. This may be thought to support the notion that the paintings were a special commission, and were never intended for general sale. It is even less likely that they were painted for non-commercial reasons: Walker appears to have lived fairly humbly, and had a large family to support; he is not likely to have had the leisure to pursue such a time-consuming hobby.

Comparison with the present state of the churches and, where relevant, with Glynne's descriptions, lends weight to the conviction that Walker was an accurate recorder of the churches of his day. I hope that publication here of some of Walker's work may lead to the discovery of further information about this elusive artist.

The Church Notes for Herefordshire

Bromyard [96.30] S. Peter 1824, 1843, 1873

This is a large church consisting of a nave with side aisles of equal height without a clerestory, a north and south transept scarce extending beyond the body, a chancel, and a low embattled tower rising from the centre. The principal part is Early English, but there are very fine Norman doorways on each side of the nave. <The two Norman doorways are remarkably lofty and grand.> The northern one is stopped up, but is very large and rich in ornament, and is set upon a kind of very shallow porch – it has three ranges of bold mouldings enriched with the chevron, lozenge and other ornaments, the head of the arch is filled with sculpture and the shafts have rich capitals. The inner arch within the Norman one is pointed. The south doorway has four tiers of moulding with the chevron, lozenge and embattled ornaments and shafts. Above it is a stone tablet on which is represented St. Peter. <The three west gables are wide, the aisles having separate roofs but the three windows are poor, one of three, two of two, lights. Most of the windows of the nave are poor. At the end of the north transept is one of three lights, plain Decorated. The south transept has a high roof and gable and a Perpendicular two-light window set above the others.> Part of the north wall seems to have been rebuilt and contains plain two-light windows without feathering, possibly modern insertions. In the south aisle are several early Curvilinear windows of two lights. There is one lancet window in the south transept and in the northern a window of a single light of this form [*sketch*]. The south transept is loftier than the nave: much of the roof is modern and of slate. The tower is very plain and low, and has a turret at the north-east angle. <The tower is low and massive, with plain battlement and a turret rising above the parapet at the north-east – circular except at the top.> The interior is handsome and well pewed. The nave has on each side a row of five pointed arches, with eight circular pillars, with square bases – the capitals are enriched with foliage, and some are octagonal. The tower rises from four plain pointed arches occupying the centre of the cross. The chancel has had all its windows modernized. <The chancel looks as if it had been wholly rebuilt. There is an adjunct on the north of the chancel for [a] vestry.> The font is of cylindrical form projecting in the centre part, and of Norman character with the scroll ornament. In the north transept is a moulded area in the wall for a tomb and in the external wall of the south transept are two monumental arches, one of which has the mouldings enriched with the ball flower.

There is a small barrel-organ in the west gallery.

The carving of the north doorway is a 19th-century imitation of Norman work. The figure of St. Peter above the south doorway is probably of Saxon origin. The capitals of the south arcade have trumpet-scallop carving dated to c.1190, while those of the north show stiff-leaf foliage c.1210.

Dilwyn [96/25] S. Mary the Virgin [before 1840]

This church is a very good structure of various styles and presenting several portions of fine workmanship in the Early English and Curvilinear styles. The church consists of a nave with narrow aisles, a north transept, chancel and a square tower of massive proportions crowned by a leaden spire, and singularly placed not in the centre of the west front but at the west end of the south aisle and extending also along half the breadth of the nave. The tower is Early English and has three heights of windows, all of lancet form, some of which have the toothed ornament in the dripstones – the lower windows are set in small buttresses – those at the corner are flat. <The tower and the clerestory have embattled parapets, but in the other parts the parapets are plain. The windows of the aisles and the transepts are all Curvilinear, mostly of two lights, but there is one of three lights in the transept and also a small one in the form of a cinquefoil. <The dripstones of the windows are all connected in a series.> There is one of two lights at the west end of the nave in the space not filled by the tower, and therefore not in the centre. On the south side is a very elegant Curvilinear porch, having on each side two fine windows each of two lights, and between them clustered shafts from whence it was intended that the ribs of the groining should spring. The outer doorway is high with good mouldings, the inner doorway has also good mouldings and is set between two rich niches. The nave is divided from each aisle by five Early English arches, with circular pillars, some of which have chevron work in the capitals. The clerestory was originally also Early English, and some lancet windows still remain over the piers, but most of the windows are rectilinear insertions of two lights with square heads. There is a half arch at the west end of the nave opening to the tower. On the two eastern piers of the nave are moulded brackets with the tooth ornament. <[*diagram*] On the exterior this window is flanked by flat buttresses.> The roof of the nave has panneling and flowered bosses. The arch to the chancel springs from clustered shafts with octagonal capitals. Above this arch are two circular windows cinquefoiled as at Pembridge. Within this arch is a wood screen – there is another in the transept and one enclosing the east end of the south aisle. The pulpit and west gallery are of carved wood of the 17th century. In the east wall of the north transept [is] a niche with a semicircular head trefoiled, with nail heading mouldings. The chancel is Curvilinear and has all the side windows of two lights, except one trefoil lancet. The interior arch of the two windows next the east end is curiously trefoiled, and the sill of the southern window is brought down very low, forming a seat. The east window is of three lights, the tracery early but good, towards the interior set within an arch of very curious character and form. <On the <u>exterior</u> this window is flanked by flat buttresses.> In the east wall is also a square bracket with the ball flower in its moulding. In the north wall is a fine tomb of Curvilinear character, beneath a rich ogee arch with crockets and finial and a band of ball flowers – it has the effigy of a cross-legged knight, bearing a shield charged with a lion. There is a circular turret on the north side of the chancel and a small vestry with a lancet window. In the north transept is the vestige of a rich brass – there is also a slab with a cross flory. The font is of octagonal form with several bands of moulding gradually diminishing in circumference – the pedestal is square.

The Early English south arcade impinges against the apex of the tower arch – the tower originally related to an earlier nave which was demolished and replaced by the present nave in the early 13th century. Thus the tower is older than the nave, and does indeed have two Norman windows with double roll mouldings.

Moccas [96/15] before 1840

This small church offers a very good specimen of Norman work, nearly unaltered except by the insertion [of] a few windows. The exterior is finely mantled with ivy. The plan includes only a nave and chancel, the latter having a semicircular east end. The nave opens to the chancel by a fine Norman arch with chevron ornament, the chancel to the semicircular termination by a similar arch. There are two original Norman windows, and some others inserted of Curvilinear character with square heads, and containing some ancient stained glass of most brilliant colouring. In the semicircular east end are three Norman windows. The chancel contains a panneled altar tomb, upon which is the effigy of a crusader in very perfect condition, with a shield and crossed legs. In the south wall is also a plainer altar tomb and two plain pointed arches. The north and south doorways are Norman, the door itself not occupying the head of the arch which is filled with rude sculpture representing horses and other animals. The font is Norman in the shape of a circular cup.

The 'rude sculpture' above the north and south doorways has now disappeared. A photograph of the south tympanum appears in Keyser (1904), and drawings of their appearance in 1850 are reproduced in Leonard (2000). The circumstances of their disappearance are obscure.

Norton Canon [96/21] before 1840

This church stands in a lovely situation, and consists of a nave, north and south transepts, and chancel with a square tower on the north side of the west front. The whole appears to be of late date, and bad character – the walls are of brick, excepting the tower which is of stone and appears to be Early English work, with flat buttresses and trefoiled windows in the two lowest stories – the belfry windows of two lancet lights trefoiled, and below the parapet a billet cornice – and the whole surmounted by a tiled roof. Adjoining the tower is a small chapel of brick. The windows have stone mullions, the lights mostly trefoiled, but apparently of late and bad period. The west window is of three lights, as are those of the transepts. The chancel is partly modern. The font is a plain octagon.

The tower is Early English, but the chancel, nave and transepts were built in 1716, the unknown architect incorporating many late thirteenth-century windows.

Ludford [96/54] [before 1840]

This small church stands on the Herefordshire side of the Teme, opposite to Ludlow. The situation is highly beautiful, being on an eminence overlooking the river with its steep rocky banks, with [? *should read* and] the romantic town and castle of Ludlow – the churchyard is richly shaded with trees and contains some very large sycamores – on the north is an abrupt descent.

The church consists of a nave, north transept and chancel with a low square tower mantled in ivy at the west end, which has a Norman door on the west side, a window of the same character on the north now walled up, and is without buttresses. The parapet is embattled. There is also a Norman window in the wall of the tower opening to the nave. The east end of the nave has a trefoiled lancet window above the roof of the chancel – one window in the nave is of two lights without feathering, others are square-headed – in the north transept is one of the latter character of three lights with a transom and very handsome tracery. A few others are trefoiled lancets, that at the west end of the chancel is rectilinear of three lights and well restored. The transept opens to the nave by a plain pointed arch and to the chancel by a small arch set obliquely.

On the south-west side of the churchyard is Ludford House, a very picturesque old mansion, of irregular form with enriched gables and bay windows, and much mantled in ivy.

Ludford was in Herefordshire at the time of Glynne's visit, and presumably this is the reason why it was not included in Cranage's The Churches of Shropshire.

Pembridge [96.23] before 1840

This is a large and handsome cruciform church, of very regular plan and offering an elegant specimen of pure and unaltered Curvilinear work. It is also very remarkable in having no steeple attached to the body, but on the north side of the churchyard is a curious building which serves for the belfry and contains five bells. This consists of a low octagonal basement of stone, surmounted by a tiled roof, which is again crowned by a square wooden cage and turret which contains the bells and a clock. This is supported upon very strong timber framework which has a curious effect in the interior. The lower part has a large square headed doorway, and small square windows. The nave has side aisles and a clerestory, and the roofs of the whole church are tiled and the parapets plain. The windows are all good and unaltered with Curvilinear tracery. The west window is of four lights, those at the ends of the transepts of three lights and very long. <The roof is high-pitched and flagged, with good bold gables and no parapets, as usual in Herefordshire.> Those at the west ends of the aisles are also of three lights, the rest of two lights. The clerestory windows are cinquefoils within circles, one set over each pier. The north porch has a pediment flanked by plain pinnacles, and within a handsome groined ceiling: it has also fine Curvilinear windows of two lights. The outer door has plain arch mouldings. The nave has on each side six pointed arches with octagonal piers, the eastern arch on each side opening to the transepts. The transepts open into the side aisles of the nave by half arches. The west windows of the side aisles contain some fragments of rich stained glass. The chancel arch has fine deep mouldings, and springs from small clustered shafts. Above this arch are two circular windows with cinquefoils, like those of the clerestory, opening above the roof of the chancel. Within the chancel arch is part of the roodloft and its screen painted and gilt with a rich band of vine leaves and grapes, and some good panneling, but mutilated. On the south side is a staircase turret and a door opening on to the roodloft. In the north transept is a trefoiled niche, and two altar tombs, each having the effigies of a man and woman – one of the male figures is in armour, and one of the ladies has the square head-dress. The chancel has an east window of four lights, and a Curvilinear one of two lights on the south. On the north are two windows of three lights, each light being trefoiled. In the south wall is an arch for a tomb, and a trefoil niche with a shaft, and a piscina. There is much good wood carving in screen work and pews, some of early, some of late character. The font is supported on a square shaft with some columns attached to each side with good capitals and bases. The gables of the parts of the church are terminated by heads or crosses.

The bell-tower was restored in 1983–84, and is now thought to date from the early 13th century (thus antedating the present church), though with substantial later additions.

Peterchurch [96/19] before 1840

This is a very curious church of Norman work, and remarkable for its arrangement, being very long and consisting of four complete portions in succession lengthways and gradually contracting in width towards the east end. At the west end is a square tower of later date, with a plain parapet, corner buttresses and three heights of single-light windows trefoiled, the whole surmounted by a well-proportioned true spire, with windows on the alternate sides having triangular canopies with finials. The tower opens into the nave by a small pointed door. The exterior of the body is plain. The nave has a semicircular doorway at the south with chevron ornaments in the mouldings and shafts. There are also some Norman windows in different parts of the walls, and in one part of the nave arranged in two heights. There are others of lancet form, and one of Curvilinear character of two lights. The nave is of considerable length, the three other compartments eastward of it are small and open to each other by plain semicircular arches, the most western of which (opening to the nave) is much misshapen and rises from imposts with the toothed ornament upon them. On the north side of it is a staircase leading to the exterior. The second arch to the next compartment has been partly walled up and has chevron work in the mouldings – within it is a part of a wood screen. The most eastern portion or chancel has a semicircular end, but unfortunately the arch of division has been cut away. The semicircular portion has some small Norman windows, with flat buttresses set externally between them, and a rope string-course running underneath. Within this part is the original stone altar which is a curiosity rarely found. The font is Norman, of circular form, standing on steps and having round the top the rope ornament. On the south side of the nave is a trefoiled niche with a drain. The interior is very plain and bare, but the arrangement of the church is highly interesting and singular.

In recent years the spire has been taken down and replaced by a fibreglass structure.

Staunton-on-Wye [96/16] before 1840

This church stands in a most beautiful situation commanding an enchanting view over the Wye with every variety of hill and wood. It is a plain small structure consisting of a nave and chancel with a square tower at the west end surmounted by a tiled peaked roof. The tower itself is Early English divided by string-courses into three stages and a cornice of billet ornament runs beneath the parapet. The lower part projects considerably in the form of an abutment – the windows are all lancets, those of the belfry double. The nave had once a north aisle now destroyed, but two pointed arches are seen in the wall with a large circular pier. The south doorway is Norman with shafts, and the arch to the chancel is pointed. There are some lancet windows, both single and double, but the greater part are modern and very bad. The font is cylindrical and plain.

Weobly [96.27] S. Peter and S. Paul before 1840

The church is a large building of chiefly Curvilinear work and built of red stone. It consists of a nave with side aisles, north and south transepts, a chancel and a lofty and beautiful tower and spire standing at the west end of the north aisle. The steeple is very lofty, almost too much so for the body, but it is an elegant Curvilinear composition. The tower has good windows of three lights in its lowest story – but it is plain above and without belfry windows. It is surmounted by a battlement, and large crocketed pinnacles at the angles, adorned with fine pannelling. The spire is connected by flying buttresses to the pinnacles and has at its base two-light windows with triangular canopies. The exterior of the body is plain with tiled roofs and no battlement. The south porch is Early English, the outer door having its arch springing from brackets. Within the porch is a Norman doorway with chevron ornament in the arch mouldings. The west doorway* is Curvilinear, having on the exterior two bands of moulding continued all down to the ground, and each filled with the ball flower.

   *<The arch of this door presents to the interior a contracted form with two bands of moulding with ball flower, but only one continued the whole way down.> Above it is a fine early Curvilinear window of large size, with four lights of the same character with the east window of Lincoln Cathedral. On each side of this window is a cinquefoiled niche with dripstone. The windows vary very much in character.

At the west end of the south aisle are two windows, one above the other, the upper is Curvilinear of two lights, the lower has two lancets within a pointed arch. There are two other windows of Early English character on the south side, having three lancets beneath a contracted arch with the toothed ornament in its mouldings. In one the lancets are trefoiled. In the north aisle are two Rectilinear windows, one a large one of four lights containing some stained glass of rich colouring. In the north transept is one very large Curvilinear window of two lights, and one smaller of similar character with some stained glass. The nave is lofty and handsome and the view from the chancel looking west is very fine. The roof is of timber, the ribs forming square compartments, and the beams resting upon wooden brackets. There are five pointed arches on each side with octagonal pillars, and one of the northern arches has two bands of ball flower in its mouldings. The clerestory windows on the north are walled up – those on the south are Curvilinear of two lights. The north aisle is much broader and loftier than the south aisle. The transepts do not extend much beyond the aisles. The north transept contains a pew surrounded by a wood screen and a good panneled wood ceiling – also a fine canopied niche. <The south transept has Rectilinear windows.>

The chancel is mostly Early English, and opens to the nave by a high arch springing from brackets. There are some windows of two lights with plain mullions without feathering. There is one on the south consisting of three lancets with dripstones beneath a contracted arch. The east window is Rectilinear of late date. On the south of the chancel arch is a fine niche of Curvilinear character with crocketed triangular canopy and feathering – its bracket has grotesque sculpture. On the north side is a doorway that once led to the rood-loft. On the south of the chancel is an ogee arch in the wall with a plain finial, beneath it two alabaster effigies. On the north side is an altar tomb of Rectilinear character with the alabaster effigy of a knight. There is a vestry on the north side of the chancel. The font is octagonal – each face beautifully sculptured with varied panneling and tracery of Curvilinear character. In the churchyard is an ancient cross.

In the town of Weobly are many beautiful specimens of domestic architecture in wood and plaster of the 15th and 16th centuries, especially one house rich in wood carving, with projecting stones supported by carved wood brackets – the windows with good tracery and the spandrels of the doors much enriched

Bridstow [96/34] S. Bridget [No date ? 1842]

This church is in a retired spot one mile from Ross, consists of a low west tower, a nave with south aisle, and south porch, a chancel with south chapel. The tower is divided into two stages by a string course and has a moulded parapet with gargoyles. There is no west doorway – a west window is of three lights each trefoiled and rather odd in the direction of the foils. The buttresses are angular – the belfry windows of two lights appear to be Decorated.. The material is red sandstone. In the south porch is a benatura [= *stoup*] much decayed. The porch is of wood framework, the sides open and arched. There is some good wood tracery on the south door. The roofs are slated – several of the windows are modernized – and the arches between the nave and aisle are removed and replaced by modern incongruous pillars – the eastern respond remains, which has early foliage. The chancel arch is a very fine Norman one – the outer moulding has the double convex chevron, the inner the lozenge; the shafts are very large and the capitals display a mixture of scrolls and antique pattern with foliage of much beauty. The chancel is nearly as long as the nave, but less lofty; it has an aisle or chapel on the south from which it is divided by two very elegant but rather small Early English arches springing from a very slender circular column having a foliated capital. The chancel extends beyond the aisle. Its east window is Perpendicular of four lights – on the north side is one trefoil lancet and one square-headed one of two lights, of transition from Decorated to Perpendicular. There is some stained glass in the latter. On the south side is a Decorated window of two lights and a small priest's door. In the north wall of the chancel are two arched recesses for tombs. The font is a large octagon. The faces ugly. In the churchyard is the shaft of a cross on octagonal steps.

The church was substantially rebuilt by T. Nicholson in 1862; he retained the Norman chancel arch and the Perpendicular tower. The south chancel chapel which Glynne described was demolished, and the arcade in the south wall of the chancel was transferred to the north.

Weston under Penyard [96/35] 1842

The church consists of a west tower, a nave with north aisle and chancel. The whole of the external walls of the body and chancel have been rebuilt in a modern incongruous style, except perhaps part of the north wall. There are north and south porches, the northern of wood. The tower is a pretty good Perpendicular one of red sandstone – three stages in height, having a battlement, angular buttresses and two-light belfry windows. On the north side a half-octagon turret projecting with small narrow apertures. There is no west door, but a Perpendicular window of three lights. The nave is divided from its aisle by four semicircular arches with the outer mouldings having the billet ornament and head corbels. The columns are circular but not massive – the capitals have the abacus, some inverted, and one charged with grotesque heads. There is a west gallery and a modern font. All other original features have been swept away. The situation is very beautiful on a slope, beneath a woody hill but with a view over orchards and much pleasing rural scenery.

Dore Abbey [96/41] Holy Trinity and S. Mary [Undated ?1842)

The present church is the chancel and transepts of the abbey church, the nave having been destroyed. The situation in a fertile and woody valley beside clear streams is highly beautiful and well-suited to monastic seclusion.. It is a very striking and lofty structure, presenting a complete specimen of Early English work. The nave was destroyed at the Reformation and the whole church seems to have lain in ruins till 1634 when an inscription within the church records that it was thoroughly repaired and new roofed and the tower built, and also the rectory endowed by John, Lord Scudamore. Of the nave remains one pointed arch on the south side and on the north one vast circular column with inverted capital, and part of the stone groining of the south aisle remains. The transepts are large and have each an aisle on the east side. A central tower was probably intended – the present tower is rather small and rising but little above the transept roof. It rises from the east side of the south transept and is built of old materials, of plain character and was erected at the time that the church was repaired. <The date of the principal part of the [*original*] church is supposed to be 1141.> The arrangement of the choir is peculiar – the choir itself short, divided from the Lady Chapel by three arches just behind the altar and the Lady Chapel divided into two by a range of arches and columns across it – the aisles are continued to the extreme east end, but the clerestory terminates with the choir, the aisles being as it were doubled round its east end. The transepts, choir and aisles have sloping tiled roofs. The south transept has a good door with arch mouldings and dripstone, containing the toothed ornament – the buttresses are rather flat-faced. Above the door are two equal lancets, with dripstones connected by a string and a vesica piscis between their heads: these lancets are very large and with fine mouldings. In the gable are two equal smaller lancets, which as well as the lower ones are set upon a string course. The aisle of the south transept has a sloping roof and a corbel-table – which exists also in the choir and side-aisles. The tower is built rather clumsily, rising from the centre of the east aisle of the south transept. There are two plain lancets in different heights at the south end of this aisle.

The interior is very grand and imposing, though the effect is impaired by the existence of ugly and irregular pues in the transepts and centre of the cross. The choir, aisles and Lady Chapel remain open. There are four very large pointed arches in the centre of the cross, springing from clustered shafts set in recesses and having capitals of stiff foliage and square abaci. In the angles are brackets as if for intended groining. The north transept has had its end window closed up, or else from immediately adjoining the abbey buildings never had one. The transepts have a clerestory or upper tier of well-moulded lancets, and each opens to the east aisle by two fine moulded arches springing from half-octagonal shafts with rude foliage

– that on the south side has the square abacus. In the mouldings of the arches are squared flowers raised to a point in the centre as in Hereford Cathedral. The choir has on each side three fine arches of the best Early English character, the first on each side next the west is acute and narrow, with continuous mouldings – the two other arches are lower, but with very fine and deep mouldings (carried down the pier) and springing from circular shafts attached to the pier, which have extremely fine capitals of rather early character and [*word uncertain*]. <The two western arches on each side of the choir seem more recent than the rest and perhaps pierced in the original wall.> Over each arch is a single lancet clerestory window with mouldings and shafts. Behind the altar are three very elegant acute arches having deep mouldings on clustered shafts, some of which have foliated capitals. These open into the aisle which is continued behind. Above these are three unequal lancet windows with very excellent mouldings and shafts with foliated capitals of varied character. These are fitted with painted glass representing saints in the richest colours. The whole of the roof of the transepts and chancel was erected when the church was restored – the brackets of the beams are carved in a sort of Italian style, but in the transepts the supports of the beams rest upon the clustered shafts with early capitals which seem intended to support groining. There are also clustered shafts in the choir which were intended for the ribs of [the] groining. There is a wood screen at the entrance of the choir of the same character as the roof inscribed *Vive deo gratias, tote mundo tumulatus Crimine mundatus, semper transire pacatus;* armorial bearings are painted upon it. The pulpit is of the same character as the roof and the screen. <The north aisle has one of the groined compartments with a boss, and the ribs are moulded. There is a gravestone to Elizabeth, daughter of Thomas Lewis, obit 1715, Oct. 14th.>

The floor of the choir is raised above the side-aisles. The aisles of the choir are groined in stone, in rather a simple style in pointed arches which spring from clustered shafts of large size with varied capitals resembling those within the choir. There are similar arches opening from the aisles into the Lady Chapel. The windows of the side-aisles and of the Lady Chapel are single lancets which externally are surmounted by a dripstone in form of a straight-sided arch and curiously adorned with a kind of billet ornament. The buttresses are large and on the north side of the choir is a small moulded doorway and curious ironwork on the door. In the apex of the east gable of the choir are two lancet windows.

The altar is a slab of stone set upon three shafts formed of clustered columns and raised on a kind of dais. Whether this is the original altar is doubtful. The aisle behind the altar or Lady Chapel is singular in its arrangement and has a beautiful effect – it has a stone groined roof supported by a range of four very light and elegant pillars with varied capitals. The columns are formed of clustered shafts and the capitals are some foliated, some have a kind of scalloped moulding – the combination of some [should be *so*] many columns, quite a forest, has a delightful effect. There is an uncommon feature in a kind of projecting buttress being added on the east side of each of these columns, from which the shafts spring – and the responds against the east wall are stilted shafts on half-octagonal basements. In the north wall of this chapel is a trefoil-headed recess with good mouldings. There is also a mutilated monumental slab with ancient inscription almost illegible. In the south wall of the aisle are two monumental arches. In the Lady Chapel the effigy of a cross-legged knight, one of the Cliffords, and near the altar the tomb of Sir John Hoskins, obt. 1613. The font is a plain octangular bowl, on a pedestal of like form.

The aisle east of the north transept is in three divisions or chapels, the middle one containing a window with round head and the ribs of the groining with no boss. In it are two recesses, one trefoiled, one straight-sided with a flower for finial. The aisle of the south transept is all in one space – it has two trefoil-headed recesses, one with a double piscina having projecting basins – between these two niches and set above them is a smaller arched recess which may have been a credence. There is also a square recess surmounted by a toothed moulding, an almery – still used as a cupboard. There is very good groining in this aisle. <The abbey buildings were on the north of the church and considerable traces remain of their plan. Some portions are converted into farm buildings.>

Thruxton [96/37] S. Bartholomew [No date ?1842]

A small church which seems to be entirely Decorated, comprising a western tower, nave and chancel, without aisles. The original character has been very little altered and there is no stucco or plaster. The tower is small and without either buttress or string course. The parapet is embattled – the belfry window Decorated of two lights – there are other very plain narrow apertures square at the top, on the west side of the tower. There is a wooden south porch with the sides of open framework. Within it a plain pointed doorway. The chancel arch is pointed with continuous mouldings. The windows are all Decorated of two lights, with simple but good tracery varying in some respects – except the east window which is of three lights and the tracery of transition character to Perpendicular. In some of the windows are good pieces of coeval stained glass. One window on the south side has a square head. The north door is closed. The pews are sadly high. The font is an octagon bearing the date 1611 – upon a pedestal with mouldings. There are crosses upon both gables of nave and chancel.

Holmer 96/36 S. Bartholomew 1843

The church consists of a nave and chancel without aisles, and a south porch and a detached steeple on the south side. The prevailing features are Early English. The steeple is low, the lower part is of stone and has two tiers of plain single lancets – the upper story is of wood with pointed roof. The porch is of wooden framework, covered with creepers and within it rather a rude Early English doorway, the inner moulding having plain imposts. The roof is tiled – the church is long and narrow and has no architectural distinction of chancel. There is a cross on the west gable. The west window Perpendicular of three lights. The east end has three lancets ranged [*sketch*] in the early manner. There is a plain double lancet in the chancel – also, a double window of narrow lights trefoiled with ogee heads. On the south is a plain obtuse door, the string below the windows being carried over it. On the north side of the nave is a window of two obtuse-headed lights within a depressed arch, almost flat. The other windows are single lancets. The chancel has a very fine coved roof, boarded in pannels, the spandrels beneath it filled with excellent pierced tracery. The space enclosed for the altar is considerable. In the churchyard is a cross. The churchyard has the appearance of a garden, being planted with flowering shrubs and garden plants.

Wormbridge [96/38] S. Thomas 1843 [revisited 1867]

This church has a very low west tower, a nave and chancel without any division. The tower is of very large dimensions though rising but little above the roof of the nave. Its character is very plain – the walls extremely thick and there are plain lancets on the north and west sides – round the base a string course. The roof of the tower is pointed, as is very common in Herefordshire. The north doorway of the nave is Norman, with two plain orders of mouldings. The external walls are stuccoed. The chancel modern. The nave has on each side plain but well-proportioned lancets. The walls are very thick. The font a plain small octagon. There are several monumental inscriptions to the Clives. The public path is on the north.

      <1867 Wormbridge church is now much improved. The church is very long but narrow and undivided. There are new open benches of oak. The roof is open and good. In the chancel one of the north windows has some excellent ancient coloured glass, with figures well preserved. The windows of the chancel are Decorated. The Early English lancets on both sides of the nave are good. The tower arch is pointed, with continuous plain mouldings. The tower has been raised and is covered by a pretty shingled spire. There is a new font of Norman design. The exterior has been cleaned of whitewash.>

Pevsner (1963) says that the church was 'violently restored' in 1851 – 59, yet Glynne in 1843 had described the chancel as 'modern'.

Much Marcle [96/49] S. Bartholomew 30 March, 1846

A fine large church, with much that is curious and good. The plan is a nave with aisles, a chancel with north aisle, and a tower situated between the nave and chancel, the aisles not passing it.

There is a good deal of First and Middle Pointed work of the Herefordshire sort and very good. The roofs are all high-pitched. <The roofs are covered with stone flags and there is a corbel-table of First Pointed character to [?] the clerestory.> The chancel is built of a grey stone, the rest of red and the north aisle stuccoed. At the west end of both aisles is a lancet – but that of the north aisle is square-headed. In the north aisle are some two-light windows of odd character, having the lights cinquefoiled and no foils in the head. In the south aisle is one similar one, one of three lights with no foils, and one three-light Third Pointed. The west window is a long Third Pointed one, of four lights, with transom – below it a door with plain mouldings. There is a south porch with high gable and plain outer door, the sides having trefoiled ogee-headed windows. Within it is a door with continuous Middle Pointed mouldings. The clerestory windows are small spherical triangles without tracery, opening to the interior by a wide splayed arch – the upper part of them is just seen externally above the aisle roof. Those on the south are enclosed. The nave is lofty and handsome within. On each side is a First Pointed arcade of four bays – the arches large, the columns massive and circular, with capitals moulded, but having some foliage. The roof is coved. The tower is Third Pointed, three stages in height, embattled, with a two-light belfry window and below it a trefoiled single opening. The tower opens internally to the nave and chancel by large arches with continuous mouldings. The tower is open within to a considerable height and has two tiers of Third Pointed windows. <There is a west gallery with a finger-organ.> The chancel and its north chapel have separate roofs and good eastern gables surmounted by crosses – there is also one on the west end of the chapel. The two east windows are of a kind not unfrequent in Herefordshire, but not elegant. They are of three lights, the two lateral ones arched but not foiled, the middle one not even arched. It is probably of transitional character from First to Middle Pointed – below both of them externally are small buttresses with triangular-headed setoffs. The chancel and its chapel seem to be contemporaneous – the arcade between them is First Pointed and has two acutely pointed arches, with [a] very light central column having a round moulded capital and octagonal base. The windows on the north and south of the chancel are mostly Third Pointed. The chancel and its chapel contain some very sumptuous and beautiful sepulchral monuments. In the latter are two fine Third Pointed tombs : (1) An altar tomb with finely panneled sides, of unequal width and feathered, and angel figures bearing shields on the larger ones; shield only on the smaller. The knight's head reclines on a helmet – he has a collar and studded belt, his feet on a lion. The lady's feet rests on two collared dogs, with a fine mantle and necklace: the head-dress of network studded with jewels – and two odd little figures supporting the head which rests on a cushion. The execution of the sculpture is very beautiful. (2) A large marble tomb also Third Pointed to Sir John Kyrle, with two rich alabaster figures of a knight and lady – a porcupine at the knight's feet. (3) In the north wall of the chancel is a very curious tomb of transitional from Middle and Third Pointed, the canopy of which forms three sides of a hexagon and is singularly panneled with sloping groining on the under side – the cornice wavy with heads over shields. The effigy is of a lady in what appears to be a religious habit, with flowing drapery, a rosary in her hand and a dog at her feet. The tomb is panneled with shields.

There is a reredos of Jacobean work. The font has a large cylindrical bowl diminishing, with band round it, upon a square plinth and round steps. There is another sepulchral effigy of a knight, cross-legged, with surcoat buttoned and a dog at his feet. <The armour studded – dog at feet – angels at head; probably of 15th century.> In the churchyard on the east side is an ancient cross.

The effigy and tomb in the north wall of the chancel is to Blanche Mortimer, Lady Grandison, c.1360 – 70. This is the finest monument in any Herefordshire parish church. The effigy of the 'cross-legged knight with surcoat buttoned' is of oak, one of only two wooden effigies in Herefordshire (cf. Clifford).

Colwall [96/48] S . James 1846

This church consists of a nave with south aisle, a chancel and a large tower on the south side of the west front, encroaching into the aisle, and a south porch. The chancel has on the north two Norman windows, on the south two lancets. The tower is very strong and massive, cutting off part of the west gable of the aisle. It is of plain character, with an embattled parapet but no pinnacles, the belfry window of two lights, in the other stages no other openings but slits. Its character is doubtful, but probably Third Pointed. It resembles in its plain and strong character other Herefordshire towers. On its east side, communicating with the porch, is a plain p[ointe]d arch doorway. The porch is of wood, within it is a Norman door having a curious segmental arch, the outer member having shafts. The east and west windows of the south aisle are both single lancets. Some other windows of the nave are Decorated of two lights and small size; others have been altered to Perpendicular. The nave is divided from the aisle by five plain Early English arches, with light circular columns having moulded capitals, one of which has some Early English foliage. The west respond has on the capital a grotesque head. The chancel arch is plain and chamfered. The east window a wide modern one. The font has a circular bowl upon a cylindrical stem. The altar chairs and pulpit have Jacobean carving. There is a west gallery, and some remains of stained glass. The roofs are tiled, the external walls of the body are chiefly stuccoed. In the chancel is a mural monument with a brass to Elizabeth, wife of Anthony Harford of Bosbury, obt. 1590. In the churchyard is the shaft of cross having hollows or niches upon it.

The chancel was rebuilt in 1865, and a north aisle added in 1880.

Little Hereford [96/55] S. Mary [Undated ?20 April 1846]

Has a nave and chancel and a massive western tower which last is an early First Pointed specimen, with thick walls and no buttresses covered with a pointed roof of tiles. <The tower is a very good plain specimen of a First Pointed tower unmixed. There is a plain corbel-table under its roof.> It has three stages – in the lowest on the west side is a doorway obtusely pointed with imposts and no shafts. The three stages are divided by string-courses – the second has a plain lancet on each side, except the north. The belfry story has two rude and plain lancets on each side without mouldings or shafts. The arch from the tower to the nave is pointed, with three orders of moulding – the inner of which has a circular shaft with moulded capital, the other imposts. The nave has on the north one small Romanesque window set high in the wall, and on the south a lancet. On each side of the nave next the chancel are Middle Pointed windows of two lights – that on the south carried down low after the fashion of a "lychnoscope": also two mutilated windows on the south. The chancel arch is small and low, of pointed form and quite plain, opened in a large mass of masonry. Near it on the south appear the brackets for fixing the rood-loft. In the south wall of the nave is a fine sepulchral arch of Middle Pointed character, having elegant cinquefoil feathering and surmounted by a triangular canopy with finial and ball-flower crockets. In the space between the canopy and the arch below is a trefoil-headed niche and the whole is flanked by square pedestals ending in triangular heads, above which seem to have been niches. There are traces of ancient colour, but the whole is much hidden by pues. The south door of the nave is First

Pointed, with mouldings like that in the tower. The chancel is interesting – has on the north and south next the nave a wide trefoil-headed lancet much splayed and near the altar a two-light Middle Pointed window on each side. The east window has been modernized. Under the south-east window is a curious piscina with projecting stone ledge having a quatrefoil-shaped orifice in the angle of the wall. The arch over it of segmental form. There are also (west of the window) three equal sedilia of plain character with trefoil heads and no shafts. In the north wall are two fine sepulchral arches somewhat resembling that in the nave, and similar to each other. The canopies ogee with crockets and finial – the feathering very bold – and flanked by octagonal pedestals with canopied sides. In the eastern arch is an incised slab with figure of a lady with hands joined in prayer. The whole very damp and covered with green mould. The chancel roof is very [?] rude timber work. There is a south chancel door and a pue enclosed by twisted wooden columns of Jacobean character. A small modern font is in use, but close to it may be seen the old one, disused for its holy purpose and filled with rubbish. In April 1846 it contained a coal shovel, bits of broken glass, dead leaves and a non-descript iron tool. This font is Romanesque – a large cylindrical bowl on base of like form.

The external walls of this church are whitewashed.

Orleton [96/57] 20 April, 1846

This church has a nave and chancel without aisles, a north porch and a low western tower crowned by a shingled spire, occupying the whole square of the tower. There are features of different styles. <In Orleton churchyard is part of a fine cross raised on steps and much resembling that at Burford. These are often to be found in Herefordshire.> The tower is very plain, as often occurs in Herefordshire, and without buttresses. It is divided by a string into two parts, the lower part has a Romanesque character with a semicircular-arched door having continued mouldings – above which is a lancet. On the south is a round-headed window – the belfry story has on each side two narrow square-headed lights very plain. There is a plain pointed south door with hood. The roof tiled and of high pitch. The north porch of wood, of Jacobean character but picturesque and covered with ivy. On the east gable of the nave is a Maltese cross. The chancel is First Pointed – the east window of two lancets – on the north and south are single ones deeply splayed. The chancel arch pointed, with continued mouldings. The rood-loft with its screen remains, but of plain character. The windows of the nave are chiefly Middle Pointed of two and three lights. One on the north has the tracery often seen in Salop and Herefordshire of three lights and has some good fragments of stained glass. The font a fine Romanesque one, now placed in the chancel, has a cylindrical bowl, sculptured with round arches springing from shafts and containing figures. The church is disfigured by pues.

The font is the work of the Herefordshire School.

Leintwardine [96/59] SS. Peter and Paul 20 April, 1846

A fine large church, comprising a nave with aisles and north chapel – a spacious church with north aisle, and a large tower on the south side of the nave, forming a porch in its lower portion. There is much of the Herefordshire character of solidity and also of the local peculiarities as to architecture and arrangement. There is some variety in the architectural features. The west door is Norman but not on a grand scale with shafts having foliated capitals. At the west end of the south aisle is a single lancet and over it a square-headed slit. At the west end of the north aisle is no window at all. The west window of the nave is of four lights with poor late tracery. The north aisle has a moulded parapet, as also the clerestory of the nave; the south aisle is embattled – the north chapel of the chancel has a high-pitched flagged roof. The tower encroaches on the aisle as at Presteigne and is of plain massive character with a battlement and Third Pointed belfry window of two lights – square-headed on the east and west sides – the other openings of the tower are small and narrow – one on the south trefoil-headed. The door [has] continuous mouldings and is probably Middle Pointed – at the north-west angle a circular stair-turret.

The windows of the south aisle are Middle Pointed of two lights – those on the north Third Pointed – some square-headed and the clerestory windows are of the latter kind. The south door within the porch is fine First Pointed, with good mouldings and broken shafts with moulded capitals. The nave is lofty and has a panelled ceiling with ribs and foliated bosses – the aisles are ceiled. The arcades of the nave are First Pointed of five bays – the columns on the north are octagonal – those on the south are circular, with moulded capitals. The north transept opens by a pointed arch upon octagonal shafts within which is a wood screen. There is a block corbel-table inside the aisle roofs. The nave is unhappily fitted up in a conventicle fashion with large gallery, canopied [?] pews and a huge pulpit in the centre of the nave near the chancel arch which it completely masks. <In the gallery an organ, erected in 1838.> Moreover the chancel arch is filled up and the chancel quite out of sight and disused. The chancel arch is pointed, on octagonal piers.

The chancel in its neglected and decaying state presents a still more melancholy sight than the true [?] conventicle look of the nave. The ancient stalls and desks remain though in wretched condition and are of fine woodwork. <There is fine ogee canopy and tabernacle work in the stalls and screen and the misericux are still extant.> The chancel is wider than the nave and has a clerestory on the south with square-headed Third Pointed windows and on the south-west side is a lynchoscope in form a lancet with trefoil head. There is an arcade of three bays between the chancel and its north chapel which is walled up and the chapel appropriated to various unworthy purposes. The arches are nearly straight-sided with octagonal piers.

<The east window of the chancel is of four lights with transom, much mutilated – under it are two recesses, one square-headed, one arched, for aumbryes.> The east ends of chancel and chapel have equal gables with Third Pointed windows of four lights. On the south side of the chancel is a curious door, of which the head is in form a round trefoil with mouldings following its form – in the same wall are two sepulchral recesses, one of which has an obtuse arch. The tombs have disappeared. The south-east window of Middle Pointed style is mutilated. In front of it are three sedilia, equal, with three foiled heads and continuous mouldings of the same style. <One of the sedilia is now made into a cupboard.> Also a singular piscina of a kind of cinquefoil form with a shelf. In the east wall is the trace of a late yet fine stone reredos, with panneling, small battlements and pinnacles. <The chancel is ceiled and the windows much broken.>

The north aisle and chapel has an open timber roof and forms school, vestry and coal-hole! It has a Third Pointed window on the west side and an arch once open to the aisle of the nave.

The font has a plain octagonal bowl, the lower part chamfered, on a square basement raised on steps.

Radical changes in 1865 wrought great improvement in the state of Leintwardine church.

Aymestrey [96/57] S. John and S. Alkild [*sic*] 20 April, 1846

An interesting church, with some local peculiarities. The plan is the usual one with aisles to the nave and a large west tower. There is a mixture of the pointed styles but no Norman. The tower is very remarkable and seems always to have formed the principal entrance to the church. <This steeple appears to be Third Pointed – is well-preserved and built of fine stone.> It has every appearance of having been used for purposes of defence, a characteristic not uncommon in the steeples of the Border country. The lower part is rudely vaulted in stone and forms the entrance. In the ringing floor above it the north and south windows outwardly are narrow slits, but much splayed internally and with window seats. The western one has two trefoil-headed narrow lights. <There are six bells and a barrel-organ.> There are corner buttresses and a stair-turret at the north-east. The walls are very thick and in the eastern wall is only a pointed door opening to the nave. In the lower part, or entrance, is a benatura [= *stoup*]. The outer door has a strongly-built pointed arch with continuous chamfer. The tower is embattled and the belfry windows of two lights. <There is a plain south porch.> The south aisle has [a] sloping tiled roof – the nave on the south is embattled – and the clerestory windows which are of two trefoiled lights, are barely seen externally. The north aisle is leaded as is the chancel. The windows of the aisles seem to be Third Pointed – square-headed with two cinquefoiled lights. – there are none at the west ends of the aisles which have solid walls. The east window of the south aisle is of two lights – Middle Pointed verging to Third Pointed. The arcades are singular, and rather coarse – on each side of the nave are three rather plain pointed arches – the piers formed each of four shafts clustered in a square form and small octagonal ones between them, the capital a general octagonal one, the bases square, the responds are of similar character. The clerestory windows present to the interior a containing arch and are probably Middle Pointed. The roofs are ceiled. The chancel arch is a plain pointed one springing from a kind of pilaster with square capital and small shafts in the angles. There is a very good rood-loft with screen, of which, however, the tracery has disappeared except immediately over the holy door; under the loft is elegant groining and overhanging foliations. There are very fine cornices of vineleaf and grapes.

The east end of the aisles is enclosed by Third Pointed wood screens. At the north-west angle of the nave is a circular turret staircase communicating with the tower. The chancel has a small east window of two lights which seems Third Pointed: on the north are no windows open – on the south they are of two lights with contracted arches of two lights. There is no lychnoscope. On the south is a small piscina with ogee head and a projecting octagonal basin. Against the south wall is a Norman capital. In the church is an incised slab with figures of a knight and lady under triangular crocketed canopy – a dog at his feet – and part of the legend remaining. The font has a circular cup-shaped bowl on a cylindrical stem attached to the north-west pier of the nave. The pulpit is Jacobean.

The situation of this church is beautiful in a narrow woody valley.

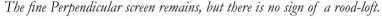

The fine Perpendicular screen remains, but there is no sign of a rood-loft.

Lyonshall [97/1] S. Michael 21 April, 1846

This church has a nave with aisles, a small north transept, chancel, south porch and west tower. The nave has a clerestory and together with the aisle has sloping roof of stone slates. There is a sancti bell-cot at the east end of the nave, having a trefoiled arch and surmounted by a cross. The porch has lancet windows, an obtuse outer door, and an inner one of plain pointed character. The lower part of the tower seems early and has two lancets on the south side, the upper part is modern, built in 1822. The prevailing features are First and Middle Pointed – the nave has an arcade of six pointed arches on the north and five on the south, the western bay on which side is walled and has trace of an early window. The piers on the north are clustered and decidedly First Pointed with four large and four small shafts – the former with moulded capitals, the latter terminating above in a sort of fleur de lys. The southern piers are octagonal. The west end of the north aisle has a small Norman window. The north transept is little more than an extension of the aisle in one bay. The clerestory windows have trefoil-headed lancets, some of which are altered or closed, and some open into the aisle below its roof. At the east end of the north aisle is a trefoil-headed lancet and there are some of the same character set singly, in pairs or in threes in the north and south aisles. The chancel arch is pointed, springing straight from the wall; and over it are two small windows with square heads, one divided by a mullion. There is a stone bracket which seems to have sustained the rood-loft. The chancel has an east window of three lights of a common Herefordshire pattern of three plain lights within a containing arch, and the whole surmounted by an arch which forms a kind of shoulder [*diagram*]. There are on the north and south of the altar two trefoil-headed lights contained in an arch resembling that just mentioned, probably early Middle Pointed, and nearer the west are two-light ones of Third Pointed period. There is wainscoting at the east end so that it is not clear whether there is a piscina. <Near the east end of the south aisle is a piscina with trefoil head.> There is a priest's door on the south side. The tower arch is low and pointed on imposts. The font is a curious First Pointed one – the bowl following the shape of the eight clustered shafts which support it and have foliage capitals, being set in a circle. There is an organ in a west gallery. The exterior has a picturesque contour and is much mantled in ivy. There is part of the effigy of a knight set against the porch externally.

In the west wall of the nave high above the tower arch is a tall Norman window which was originally in the west wall of a former tower, but now opens into the present tower. Pevsner states that the west bay of the south arcade was only opened at the time of a restoration in 1872; until then it had been solid.

Yazor [97/2] S . John 21 April, 1846

The ancient parish church, now deserted since the erection of a new one in another site, is rather a curious building consisting of a nave with short south aisle, south transept, north porch and west tower. The tower is low but very massive and has a saddleback roof, the gabled sides being boarded. There are large buttresses on the south and west, and no door – there is no belfry window on the north – on the west a square-headed one. The north porch is of wood and very pretty, with feathered bargeboards and a pierced trefoil in the pediment above the doorway. There are very few windows. On the north side of the nave is one of two trefoil-headed lights. At the west of the south transept is a double lancet – on its south side one of three trefoil-headed lights within a continuous arch. At the east two trefoiled lights with a quatrefoiled circle over them, but no hood. Near it are image brackets. There is an arcade of three pointed arches with octagonal piers between the nave and aisle – of which the transept may be called an extension. The chancel arch is very odd – one half being circular, the other pointed – the Norman portion having a plain impost moulding. The chancel has on the north a small Norman window – at the south-east a lancet, at the south-west a lychnoscope, which is a trefoiled lancet. The east window resembles that of Lyonshall. There is a wall between the aisle and the transept on which is a low pointed arch. The south door of the nave has ball-flower in the mouldings. The roofs are sloping and tilted. In the churchyard is a very fine yew tree.

The old church at Yazor, described above by Glynne, now stands in ruins. The new church had been built in 1843 by George Moore; it is now closed for worship, but is in the care of the Churches Conservation Trust.

Mansel Lacy [97/3] S. Michael 21 April, 1846

A neat Herefordshire village church consisting of a nave with south aisle, a chancel, south porch and west tower. There are many of the features described in the last-mentioned churches [*i.e. Lyonshall and Yazor*], especially in the windows, and the prevalent character is First and Middle Pointed.

The tower is rather small, having a pointed tiled roof, divided by string-courses into three stages. On its south side is a door, over which is an early string-course with block corbels. The tower has no buttresses. On its west side are two heights of trefoil-headed lancets – the belfry windows on each side have two lights slightly ogeed and trefoil-headed. The windows of the church seem to be chiefly of two lights and of the early Middle Pointed character so often seen in Herefordshire [sketch]. The east window of the south side is of three lights of the latter sort. Those in the chancel are of two lights very similar, but have containing arches and one has a lozenge above the lights. The east window is of the form already noticed as prevalent in the county – of three lights simply with mullions and no tracery – the centre being very flat – the lateral ones lancet-headed – but this one is remarkable from the mullions and moulding being entirely covered with ball-flowers, which elegant ornament contrasts curiously with the crude design of the window and at the same time marks it to be of Middle Pointed work.

The roofs are flagged and high-pitched without parapets, and the chancel is very nearly equal in length to the nave.

The south porch has a plain outer door – a ribbed coved roof with embattled cornice – and an inner door of flattened trefoil form, near which is an octagonal benatura [= *stoup*].

The nave has a low arcade of three pointed arches, with octagonal piers – the eastern pier has a large piece of walling which is perforated with a rude aperture of flattened trefoil form and also with a long oblong recess having the appearance of an aumbrye. There is also a hagioscope in the same wall. <The bases of the piers have a kind of wedge at the alternate sides so as to make them almost quadrangular.> The east window of the south aisle has the sill extended and the jambs oddly excavated, indicating the former existence of an altar. On the north of it is an arched piscina – on the south a square corbel something like a cushion capital. On the north is also what appears to be a sedile. The tower opens to the nave by a contracted arch having now the appearance of a window, and on the north there is a flattened trefoil-shaped door leading to a staircase.

The chancel arch is pointed upon octagonal shafts. The chancel has a cradle roof ribbed as generally in Devonshire. The nave is ceiled. The east window has the ball-flower in the mouldings of its upper portion. There is no sedile in the south-east window, but near it is a horizontal moulded bracket and opposite to it a similar one. The north-west window of the chancel has the jamb cut something in the same way as the east window of the south aisle.

The altar has carved legs. The pulpit Jacobean. The font is Norman – a cylindrical bowl moulded, swelling towards the base, upon two circular steps.

The benches are mostly open.

Clehonger [96/51] All Saints 22 April, 1846

The plan. Nave with south aisle, north transept, chancel and west tower. There are as usual considerable First and Middle Pointed portions. The gables are high and flagged roofs of good pitch. The tower is First Pointed, with a later battlement and belfry story. It is of four stages divided by strings, and has no buttresses; no west door; and lancets in the two lowest stages. Its arch to the nave is a very plain First Pointed one, on imposts. The south aisle is very wide and divided from the nave by an arcade of four First Pointed arches, with light circular columns with octagonal capitals and square bases. On the north side of the nave is a small two-light window without foils and one square-headed three-light one of Middle Pointed character. The north transept opens by a wide pointed arch springing straight from the wall and has one window like that described at Much Marcle, only with foliations to the side-lights, and a square-headed one (Middle Pointed) on the east side. In the east wall of this chapel is a square aumbrye very deep, over which is a moulded bracket, and there is a trefoiled piscina with projecting drain. In the transept is also a small slate altar tomb, with the effigy of a female smaller than usual, of one of the Aubry family. At her feet is a swan or pheasant biting her mantle – angels at her head – and the drapery finely executed. There are also brasses of a knight and lady – the latter with butterfly head-dress and two little dogs at her feet. On an altar tomb is a knight with shield on which are the arms barry, on bend 3 lions heads. <The armour studded – dog at feet – angels at head; probably of fifteenth century.>

The south aisle has some two-light windows without foils and at its east end the peculiar Herefordshire three-light. Within the south porch is a Norman door, the outer moulding upon shafts. In the south wall is a sepulchral arch with good mouldings under which is a slab with cross incised. There are a few encaustic tiles. The chancel arch is quite plain pointed. The chancel has on the north two lancets cinquefoiled – on the south a square-headed one of three lights like that in the transept; and one small square one nearest the west, simply mullioned. The east window as on the opposite leaf [*i.e. as drawn on the facing page*]. In the north wall are two square recesses. On the south side a three-foiled niche and a circular bowl with drain in the cill of the south-east window. There are some remains of desks of stalls [*sic*]. The font is First Pointed cylindrical, surrounded by bands, and diminishing towards the base. This is a genuine Herefordshire church, with scarcely any Third Pointed work.

Hampton Bishop [96/63] S. Andrew 22 April, 1846

The plan – nave and chancel, with north aisle to both and a tower on the north side of the nave, eastward of which the aisle begins. There is a south porch, within which is a very curious early Norman doorway. The door itself has a flattened trefoil head above which is a transom of stone with hollowed square and other early (as the scaly) ornament, the arch head has chevron ornament, the outer hood [*diagram*]. The chancel arch is a low Norman one upon imposts, without moulding and there is a similar one between the chancel and its aisle on short half-round shafts with sculptured capitals. The chancel has on the south a lancet lychnoscope and two trefoiled lancets. The east window of the chancel [is] of the kind before noted at Clehonger. The north aisle of the chancel has at the east end two trefoil-headed lancets – also one trefoil lancet and one large late debased window. On the south side of the nave is one window of two trefoil-headed lancets – a common form and some other on the same side appear Third Pointed [diagram].

The tower opens to the nave by an acute arch of First Pointed appearance – the remainder of the arcade of the nave also First Pointed with wide arches and cylindrical columns. On the north of the nave (westward of the tower) is a small Norman slit. <At the east end of the north aisle is a fine reredos with a series of seven canopied niches – also a trefoil-shaped piscina.> The tower is early, mostly stuccoed, but the upper part is of wood with pointed roof. On its west side in the lower part is a Norman slit – above on the north a very plain obtuse double window. The west window is bad. In the chancel is a piscina on the south side, in form a trefoil with moulding. The font has a cylindrical bowl on a round stem. There is a modern Gothic reredos, some poor modern stained glass and an organ – the air is admitted through open grating in the doors and the church is well cared for. The churchyard is mostly pretty – in it is the shaft of a cross upon several steps.

Mordiford [96/64] Holy Rood 22 April, 1846

A small church much modernized but in a lovely situation and the churchyard much dressed. It has a nave, chancel, north transept and chapel south of the chancel and a tower on the south side of the nave. There is a Norman south door which is tall and good – with bold chevron mouldings and shafts with [some] sort of cushion capitals. The tower is on the south of the west end, very plain with tiled pointed upper portion – it has some lancet windows but of doubtful antiquity. The north door, which is Norman, has been closed. The west window appears to be Third Pointed of three lights. There is a plain continuous arch to the chancel and to the north transept a rude obtuse one. The south chapel of the chancel is modern and very poor – several windows are modern throughout. The east window is of [the] Third Pointed Hereford kind. South of the altar is a round trefoil-headed piscina. The pulpit is inserted in the chancel arch. There is a barrel-organ. The roofs covered with the stone flags so often seen in this county. Built into the south wall is an early capital. In the churchyard a slender tall cross on steps.

The tower was built in 1811 – previously the tower was central, situated between the nave and chancel, and it was adorned with a remarkable dragon, probably painted in the 14th century. The site of the original tower is revealed by the interpolation between the nave and chancel of two arches, which were once the east and west arches at the base of the tower. The north aisle was added in the later 19th century by F.R. Kempson; the capitals are very florid, as at Bishop's Frome.

Fownhope [96/61] S. Mary 22 April, 1846

A good parish church, consisting of a nave with south aisle, a chancel, a tower with spire between the chancel and nave and on the south side of it a kind of transeptal chapel.

There is a good deal of Norman and First Pointed work in some parts mixed curiously and other portions Middle Pointed: but as usual in the county little or nothing of Third Pointed. The tower is of mixed Norman and First Pointed character and very massive – divided into three stages by string-courses, with a staircase at the north-east angle with a small door and a Norman slit in the angle. The string-course has a First Pointed character – the window of the second stage has two plain lancets under a hood; the belfry a double Norman window with shafts, set under a large semicircular arch also on shafts. The spire is shingled and very massive – just below it the tower has a chevron cornice. On the north side in the lower stage a Third Pointed two-light window has been inserted. The nave and aisle have separate high roofs, covered externally with stone flags. The south chapel has a lean-to roof. Within the north porch is a fine First Pointed doorway with good mouldings and two orders of shafts with bands. The arcade between the nave and aisle is First

Pointed, of four bays and in two divisions – there being in the centre a large pier of wall – the eastern pier circular – the western octagonal and corresponding forms of shafts attached to the large pier. The west respond is octagonal, the eastern clustered shafts terminating in points. The windows of the nave and aisle are mostly Middle Pointed of two lights, that at the west end of three lights (as opposite), a Hereford form [*diagram*]. The tower is on three arches – the western opening to the nave is Norman on large bold shafts – the eastern, opening to the chancel is pointed in form, but on shafts much resembling the other. Another later arch of pointed form and continuous is opened in the tower wall to the south chapel – which communicates also with the aisle by a smaller arch. In this chapel are two Middle Pointed windows of two and three lights. The eastern has the lights simply three-foliated. Under the south window is a square piscina with [an] 8-foil orifice. <A barrel-organ in the west gallery. In the south chapel is a Third Pointed tomb to Capel Lechmere and wife.>

The chancel has early Middle Pointed windows, of two lights and mostly without foils – the south-western has three-foiled lights and a quatrefoil above them. Under the south-eastern is a trefoiled piscina with a two-foiled orifice. The east window is of three lights and has some stained glass. In the north wall near the east end is a square recess. On each side of the chancel is an arched sepulchral recess of Middle Pointed character with ball-flower in the mouldings – but there are no effigies remaining. There is an incised slab in the chancel, the inscription on which is not easy to decypher. There is a string-course under the windows, and on the exterior, in the gable above the east window, is a small arch hooded containing a quatrefoil circle. The buttresses have generally pedimental heads. Under the west window is the trace of a Norman door – in the tympanum is some curious sculpture which appears to represent the Holy Trinity – also the figures of a bird amidst twining foliage and dragons. The font is not good – the bowl octagonal with fleur de lys, on an octagonal stem.

It is very curious that Glynne recognised that the sculpture of the tympanum represented the Holy Trinity and not the Virgin and Child; it was usually assumed to be the latter until 1953, when Boase suggested that this work of the Herefordshire School was a representation of the Trinity.

Brampton Abbots [96/66] S. Michael 22 April, 1846

A poor church; comprising only a chancel and nave with a mean belfry attic at the west end. There is a curious Norman south door – the door-head flattened trefoil, but the surrounding arch semicircular on shafts. There is a Norman window set up high on the north side of the nave and one other north of the chancel. On the south are some late windows. The western window Middle Pointed of two lights –the eastern closed. The chancel arch very odd – wide and rather straight-sided – the inner member on an octagonal jamb, the outer on early shafts facing west but on the east side merely imposts. The font has an octagonal bowl panneled with quatrefoils containing flowers, and diminishing – the lower part panneled in something of a Middle Pointed fashion. There is a small square aperture in the wall, north of the chancel arch. Over the altar is some wood carving, apparently part of the rood-loft. There is a brass thus inscribed "Orate pro a[n]i[m]abus Joh[ann] Rudhall Armig. et Johanne uxoris sue qui obiit xxiiii die Februari anno domini Mille cccccvio- quor[um] a[n]i[m]abus propicietur de[u]s Amen." There is a barrel-organ, three bells and high pues.

Eastnor [96/63] [?22] April 1846

Plan – nave and chancel, with north aisle continued along both – west tower and south porch. The walls of sandstone, and the roofs covered with the picturesque stone slate or flag so often used in Herefordshire. The porch is of wood and has some feathering. The nave is very wide – the south door Norman with one order of shafts. The tower is strongly built and rather rude, perhaps Third Pointed having a battlement – two-light belfry window and a west window of three lights of tracery early in the style. The buttresses are at the angles. The tower arch is lofty and quite open to the nave, having continuous mouldings and no capitals. The nave has three pointed arches dividing the aisle springing from octagonal columns of considerable height, with stilted bases. In the aisle are some lancet windows, deeply splayed.. At the west of the aisle an early First Pointed window having three lights simply trefoiled under a pointed arch. The chancel arch is semicircular with imposts of Norman character. Between the chancel and the north chapel or aisle is an ugly modern arch. The windows of the latter are Third Pointed of three lights and in its east wall is a trefoil-headed niche. The east window of the chancel is Third Pointed of three lights, containing painted glass executed by the Countess Somers. Some other windows have lost their tracery.

The whole of the pues formerly existing in the nave have been replaced by open benches, thanks to the right feeling of the present Earl and Countess Somers. The altar-cloth neat and a reredos inscribed with the Decalogue etc. The only pue existing still is in the chancel and the property of the Rector. There is a nice finger-organ, not exalted in a gallery. The font has a plain circular bowl upon a basin of like form, but it is doubtful whether ancient. In the north chapel is an altar-tomb, in memory of the late Earl Somers.

In 1852, Sir George Gilbert Scott rebuilt the church. He retained the 14th-century west tower, the Norman south doorway and the Early English north arcade, and designed the rest of the church in the Decorated style.

Mathon [95/64] 10 July, 1846

The plan is chancel and nave (with no aisles) and west tower. The roofs tiled. The nave has on the north side two lancets, one of which is trefoiled, and one square-headed one of two lights. On the south some modernised windows, one of two lights. On the north and south of the chancel are Middle Pointed windows of two lights – at the east end two Norman windows with a circle above them. There seems to have been a Norman door on the north side, the tympanum of which is closed, and the horizontal doorhead has the rope moulding. The south door within a porch of wood and brick is also Norman. There is no chancel arch, but the roof of the chancel is lower than that of the nave. The font is plain, having an octagonal bowl much knocked about and has some sort of foliage. The roof is plain with rude tie-beams. Several dormer windows of ugly sort have been let into the roof on the south side. On the south side of the altar is an obtuse arch with a piscina and an oblong recess on the wall. The tower is Third Pointed and not bad, surmounted by a battlement of four crocketed pinnacles which are somewhat mutilated. The belfry window on each side is of two lights – in the second stage is a narrow slit. On the west side a poor two-light window and below it a door with continuous moulding. The buttresses are angular, having on the second stage small niches.

In the churchyard on the south side is the base of a cross. Six bells.

Mathon, now in Herefordshire, was in Worcestershire at the time of Glynne's visit.

Eardisley [97/12] S. Mary September 1847

A curious church and a very good example of the Herefordshire kind. The plan is a nave with aisles and clerestory, chancel, south porch and tower at the west end of the north aisle. Both aisles and clerestory have the usual flagged sloping roofs without parapets and there is an admixture of the three earlier styles [*i.e. Norman, Early English, Decorated*], with the characteristic absence of the later [*i.e. Perpendicular*]. The tower is modern and of no style. On some of the gables are good stone crosses. The west door of the nave is closed – the outer one of the south porch is pointed upon imposts. The windows vary – in the south aisle are some square-headed ones of two lights which seem to be of Middle Pointed age – one has two ogee trefoiled lights with trefoil between them, but without a containing arch. The clerestory windows are of two such ogee trefoiled lights, but without the trefoil above. On the north side the clerestory windows no longer exist. In the north aisle they are chiefly lancets – some double – one triple and mostly trefoiled. The south aisle is narrow, the north aisle of some width. <The west window is of three lights, each trefoiled, under a hooded arch and seems to be early Middle Pointed.> The interior very interesting and presenting much variety and irregularity in its arcades.

The southern arcade has the three western arches Norman and very rude without mouldings, the piers square, with an impost moulding – the angles are chamfered and in them are set some curious heads – some others upon the pier itself mixed with foliage. On the third pier is a small arch of semicircular form, now the entrance to the pulpit – also an ogee-headed niche and a small square-headed recess by the pulpit. <The southern piers are stilted on high square bases; the third pier on this side very wide and the eastern arch on this side the broadest.>

The northern arcade has four pointed arches, of which the eastern is lower than the others, and of ogee form with a finial, the two first piers from the west are octagonal – to the next is attached [a] circular shaft with octagonal capital – the next pier has merely an impost capital and the fifth arch is moulded continuously. There is no chancel arch and an ugly gallery is built across the entrance to the chancel, in which may be traced some fragments of the rood-loft. The door and steps to the latter may be seen on the south side. The roof of the nave is lofty but ceiled. The pulpit is partly of stone – on its eastern side is a small Third Pointed niche with an embattled cornice and on its west side a small square-headed one. In the south aisle near the east end is a square recess and small pointed piscina.

The chancel is large – the east end is a Herefordshire one of three lights, the centre one not foiled, the lateral ones trefoiled and the rear arch forming a kind of shoulder. The south-east window is of two trefoil-headed lancets – the south-west is a triple lancet. There is a hagioscope from the north aisle into the chancel. The east window of the north aisle nearly resembling that of the chancel is closed. At this end of the aisle the original altar platform remains – at the north-east side are two trefoil-headed lancets.

The font is a very remarkable one of Norman character – the form is cylindrical covered with curious sculpture, amidst which may be distinguished human figures, two of whom seem to bear harps, one a cross, one a crosier – and there is one lion; the sculpture about them represents a sort of knotty work – round the upper part a chain-like ornament – round the base some knotty sculpture – and the font is set on two circular steps.

The superb font, now recognised as the work of the Herefordshire School, is now generally believed to depict the Harrowing of Hell, a well-known motif in Romanesque art, together with two knights fighting.

St. Weonard [97/16] 10 May, 1849

This church, situated on an eminence, is seen at some distance. It consists of a nave and chancel, each with north aisle, a western tower and south porch. The principal features are Third Pointed. The tower is extremely massive and of fair height, but looks bald from want of pinnacles. It has corner buttresses and a battlement –divided into three stages. There is a four-light window on the west side but no door – a modern one being inserted on the south. The belfry windows of two lights, somewhat poor – and in the second stage a single moulded window. The whole church is of the red sandstone of the country. The porch is now used as a vestry; its outer doorway has mouldings dying into the wall – its side windows are of two trefoil-headed lights. The windows in the north side of the nave are square-headed, of two, three and four lights, the smallest of which has a small-flowered moulding externally. On the south side of the nave are two trefoil-headed lancets. The nave is divided from the aisle by an arcade of four large pointed arches with octagonal columns having capitals. The tower arch has continued mouldings. The chancel arch is less lofty, but springing from octagonal shafts. The chancel opens to its aisle by one similar arch and there is a rood-screen across the entrance both to chancel and north chapel. There is no window on the south of the chancel but there is a trefoil-headed piscina. The east window of the chancel has three ugly wide lights, late Third Pointed. The north-east window is square-headed, of two lights. The east window of the north chapel is rather a good Third Pointed one, of four lights, with transom and containing some stained glass. The font is Third Pointed, having an octagonal bowl, panneled with quatrefoils. <It is of a kind not uncommon in the Diocese of Hereford.> There are a few new open benches, but several pues; and a gallery in the north aisle in which is a finger organ. There is a wood screen within the tower arch.

Langarron [97/17] S. Deinst 10 May, 1849

A church in a most pleasing situation in a rural churchyard filled with trees and surrounded by delightful rural village scenery.

It consists of a nave with north aisle, chancel, western tower with stone spire and south porch. The north aisle has been rebuilt in a modern Gothic style, not very good – and the new arcade is a bad one with four flat arches, having slight octagonal piers. <The aisle was rebuilt AD 1841.> The porch somewhat resembles that at St. Weonards, but the side-openings are square-headed and over the inner door is a mutilated niche of late date, with a depressed embattled canopy. On the south side, between the porch and the west end is a gable carried up against the roof, containing a two-light Middle Pointed window – below which is a square-headed debased one divided by a plain mullion. Another window on the south of the nave is square-headed and Third Pointed – another modernised. The chancel arch is pointed on octagonal shafts of large size with huge capitals having banded mouldings. On each side of the chancel arch is a hagioscope with square head. The north-west and south-west windows are square-headed, with one mullion and no tracery. The north-east one is Middle Pointed, of two lights. The south-east square-headed, also Middle Pointed. The east window Third Pointed of two lights, the hood having head corbels. The chancel is dark and wainscoted, and over the sacrarium is an arabesque plaster ceiling. The pulpit is Jacobean.

The steeple though plain is rather pleasing. The tower has no string-courses, but a coped moulded parapet. On the south side is a stair-turret nearly in the centre beginning in a square form and rising into an octagon, lighted by slits and continued above the coping of the tower so as to form the door of entrance to the leads. On the west side is a two-light window of Third Pointed character but no door – though there is a modern one on the south. There are corner buttresses, belfry windows of two lights, except that on the south which is single, with bold mouldings. The spire is octagonal, but not ribbed having in the lower part of alternate sides a spire light. There is a plain slit in the tower below the belfry windows. The material [is] red sandstone – and all worked very plain.

The roofs have modern slating.

One of the stones in the south-east buttress of the chancel bears a Norman knot motif.

Marstow [97/20] S. Mary 10 May, 1849

A very small church, comprising a nave and chancel only, with south porch and a bell-gable over the west end with two open arches for bells. There is no chancel arch but the chancel is lower than the nave. The porch is very plain, with stone benches and pointed doorways. On the north side of the nave is one trifoliated lancet – and one of two lights which seems transitional from Middle to Third Pointed. On the south is a labeled Third Pointed window of two lights. The east window is Middle Pointed of three lights. On the north of the church is a single trifoliated lancet, on the south a double one. The interior is much choked up with pues. The pulpit is Jacobean. The font is a plain octagonal one. The external walls are whitewashed – the roofs covered
with stone tiles.

The church was rebuilt in 1855 by T. Nicholson.

Goodrich [97/19] S. Giles 10 May, 1849

A plain church, consisting of a nave and chancel, undivided, with co-extensive north aisle – a western tower with spire, and south porch. The steeple is singularly plain, and is without buttresses or windows deserving the name, there being no openings but small slits. The spire is lofty and octagonal – of broach kind occupying the square of the tower and having canopied lights in the lower part on the alternate sides. The nave has a First Pointed arcade of four arches rather plain, but the eastern one having rather better mouldings. There are two circular First Pointed piers, but the western pier is octagonal. The western respond is octagonal, dying into the wall. There is no chancel arch – the chancel is of two bays and has two odd-looking arches, nearly straight-sided with octagonal piers, probably of Middle Pointed character. In the eastern arch is an ancient altar tomb having the sides panneled with First Pointed arches springing from shafts with capitals of foliage. All the lateral windows of this chancel are modernized and bad. At the west end of the north aisle is a Middle Pointed one of three lights. The two east windows are Third Pointed – both of five lights, but differing in character. The porch has an arched door on the east side as well as in the usual place – and on the west a two-light Middle Pointed window. The outer doorway has continuous mouldings – the inner one has been modernized. The interior is pued – and galleried on the south and west, the latter containing an organ. The font is a very poor little modern one.

Walford [97/21] S. Leonard 10 May, 1849

An interesting church, consisting of nave with north aisle, chancel with north aisle, north and south porches and a tower on the north side of the aisle of the chancel. The styles are mixed – the nave is very wide, but the aisle is narrow, with a lean-to roof – the arcade of the nave is a very good First Pointed one, of four arches with circular columns which have varied circular capitals, some with foliage, some with the bold semi-Norman ornament which it is difficult to describe <*sketch*> – the east respond is flowered. The aisle has no windows on the north but a plain splayed lancet at the west is an odd one, of two lights, with transom and very long. The west window of the nave in its appearance Flamboyant, but questionable whether altered or not. The chancel arch is pointed, upon shafts – above it are several brackets. The windows on the south side of the nave are bad modern ones. Between the north aisle of the nave and that of the chancel is a small plain First Pointed arch upon corbels with octagonal caps – the rood-stairs remain on the north side of the chancel arch, the entrance from the aisle. The chancel has on the south three single ogee lights cinquefoiled. The east windows both of chancel and aisle are Third Pointed of three lights. Between the chancel and north aisle is an arcade of three elegant little arches, which though of First Pointed period are semicircular and spring from very slender circular columns, with moulded capitals. The eastern bay is walled and at the east end is a raised platform for an altar. There is a lancet window on the north side. On the south side of the chancel is a deep piscina with pointed arch and square projecting basin and a sedile on the north side which is trefoiled.

The roofs of the church have tie-beams. The tower is connected with the aisle by a short passage and is plain – probably First Pointed with buttresses to the lower part only – and a battlement – the belfry windows plain lancets, the other openings mere slits. The font is Third Pointed, the bowl octagonal, panneled alternately with quatrefoils and rich roses in squares: the roses are also on the slope below the bowl and the stem. The south porch has an open roof – stone benches and two-light Third Pointed windows. The north porch is rather superior to it – its outer arch of better character.

There is a lych-gate – from the churchyard an enchanting view.

Cradley [97/14] S. James 16 May, 1849

This church comprises a long wide nave and chancel, without aisles, a western tower and south porch. The porch is a pretty picturesque specimen of wood framework of rather late character. Within it is a Norman doorway with cylindrical and chevron mouldings and shafts. There is no architectural distinction of chancel. Some windows are modern and bad. On the south of the nave near the pulpit, is a narrow Norman one. Some others are Middle Pointed, of two lights, and one a trifoliated lancet on the south near to the west end. At the south-east corner of the nave is a piscina, of ogee form trifoliated, the orifice octofoiled. The base of the wood screen still remains, with some wood carving. The church has been much modernised – the chancel is lower than the nave and has an ugly plaster ceiling. The tower is very massive – the lower part is First Pointed, and opens to the nave by a fine arch of two moulded orders, with clustered shafts which are keeled and have early foliage in the capitals. On the north and south are lancet windows – on the west a Third Pointed one of three lights. The belfry story is of a different stone and Third Pointed, with a plain bold battlement. There are corner buttresses.

The east window is a wretched modern one – over it, externally, are some head corbels. The north side has very few windows. The font bears the date 1712, and presented by the celebrated Dr. Bisse. Though ugly, it has a drain. There is a lych-gate and a beautiful view from the churchyard over orchards in fine blossom.

In 1868, the chancel was rebuilt by Sir George Gilbert Scott, and in 1869 a north aisle was added and the nave substantially rebuilt by A.E. Perkins. The tower and the south doorway from the previous church survive.

Castle Frome [97/15] S. Michael 18 May, 1849

A small church in a secluded spot. It consists only of nave and chancel, with a belfry of wood over the west end. There are several Norman features – both the west and south doorways which are very narrow and plain – with a horizontal stone transom between the doorhead and the arch. On both doors, especially the southern, is some curious ancient iron work. There is a wooden porch on the south with open framework, but debased in character. On the north side of the nave are two small narrow Norman windows, and there is one of like kind on the north of the chancel; and one at the west end of the nave. The chancel arch is also Norman, rather wide, with square-edged orders and impost mouldings. The roof of the nave is flat, with plain ribs. On the south is a three-light window of Third Pointed character. The nave is much encumbered with pues. <In this church is the following inscription to Wm. and Eliz. Stone 1703:

> What poets figured Deucalion once did do
> Time here will in reality prove true
> Ston
> And never moulder into dust again
> But with the beryl and the jasper mixt
> Shall in the new Jerusalem be fixt.>

The chancel has a Third Pointed east window of three lights, with some remains of stained glass. The south-west window of two lights seems also Third Pointed; the south-east window is Middle Pointed of two lights and very remarkable for a small effigy of a knight in chain armour, holding in his hand a heart, at the base of the mullion – a feature which is perhaps unique. Under this window is an obtuse arched recess in the wall, with hood on corbel heads. Eastward of it is a square recess in the same wall. There is a nice panneled ceiling over the sacrarium, with slender ribs and very fine bosses, and also a moulded beam flowered. Against the east wall is a large monument, temp. Charles I, of rather good sculpture for the time, with effigies of a man and woman, and the sons and daughters below, kneeling at faldstools, commemorating some of the family of Unitt.

The font is the grand feature of this church and one of the finest of the kind existing. It is Norman, the bowl circular, bearing rich Norman sculpture, representing the Evangelistic symbols, the Baptism of Our Saviour – round the upper part a course of intersecting scrolls and at the base are three broken figures, one of which is armed – but it seems doubtful whether they belonged to the font originally. It is set upon a circular step.

The font is now recognised as one of the outstanding works of the Herefordshire School.

Linton [97/23] S. Mary 17 May, 1850

The church is situated high, in a charming site, within a churchyard shaded by fine trees. It consists of a nave with aisles, a chancel long in proportion, a western tower with stone spire, and north porch. The nave and aisles are comprehended under one roof. There is a mixture of styles, but a good proportion of the earlier ones, all however are of a plain character. The arcades are irregular. On the north are two very plain Norman arches (not including the western bay which is walled from the nave and forms a vestry). One [pier is] circular with Norman indented capitals, the eastern one square – all clumsy and not well fitted to the arches. There is a third arch on the north next the chancel, which is very small and narrow, but of semicircular form. The south arcade has three wide pointed arches, springing from First Pointed circular pillars. The aisles are very narrow. The interior dark and dingy – and very much encumbered with hideous pues. The chancel arch is pointed and continuous. The east window is, oddly enough, a single lancet with the head squared. On the south of the chancel are two doublets each with trefoiled head; and at the north-west of the chancel a two-light Middle Pointed window.

In the south aisle is one Middle Pointed window of two lights – the others debased and square-headed. The tower arch is pointed, springing from cylindrical shafts: the tower has fair stone groining within – the bell aperture curiously fringed with foliage. The steeple appears to be Third Pointed. The tower has a moulded parapet and is surmounted by an octagonal spire with ribs at the angles, but no spire lights. The west doorway is pointed – the hood on corbels. The west window debased. In the next stage a single square-headed light with trefoiled ogee. The belfry windows differ. That on the west has a Middle Pointed look – those on the north and south decidedly Third Pointed – on the east Flamboyant. There are corner buttresses and an octagonal stair-turret on the north-east not reaching above the first stage.

The north porch is plain – the most frequented path to the church from the village lies through the north side of the churchyard. The font is modern.

Upton Bishop [97/25] S. John 17 May, 1850

This church has a nave with south aisle, chancel, western tower and south porch. The latter is used as a vestry. There are, as usual, some early features and some of later date. On the north side of the chancel is one long lancet (next the west) and eastward of it a double window with ogee heads trefoiled – externally exhibiting coarse finials and a head in the space between the heads – the whole enclosed under a square head. The nave has a First Pointed arcade of early character – the arches pointed and quite plain, the pillars cylindrical, with abaci to the capitals, one of which has a sort of indented Norman ornament, the other rude foliage. The chancel arch is a plain pointed continuous one. The east window of the chancel is Middle Pointed of two lights and there are two others of the same sort on its south side. At the east end of the aisle is a poor Gothic window, over which is a trefoil-headed lancet in the gable. On the south side of the nave are square-headed windows of three lights of Third Pointed character – the lights ogeed and trefoiled. The nave extends a little beyond the aisle. The font has an octagonal bowl, diminishing to a shaft of like form. The tower is Third Pointed with parapet moulded but not embattled and coarse buttresses which become smaller at the belfry story. The belfry windows are of two lights – in the next stage is a single square-headed one. On the west side a large and good one of four lights, the hood upon corbel-heads. On the north is a square-headed labeled window in the second stage.

There is a lancet window at the west end of the aisle.

Glynne does not mention the part of a Roman tombstone embedded externally in the south wall of the chancel; it shows the head, shoulders and raised arm of a man set in a recess. South of the chancel is a hexagonal vestry built in memory of Frances Ridley Havergal (1836 – 79), the famous Victorian hymn-writer, sister of the then incumbent.

Dynedor [97/35] S. Andrew 21 May, 1851

A small and rather mean church – having nave and chancel, north porch and low square tower at the west end. The latter may possibly be debased and has a pointed tiled roof: no western doorway – the belfry window square-headed, of two lights – and below one of a single light. In the belfry window is some brick lattice-work. The tower arch opening to the nave is low and poor. On the south side of the nave is a First Pointed window, looking more like one in a belfry – of two lights, with central octagonal shaft with rude capital and base. Between the heads a trefoil and the whole included in a pointed label or hood. The chancel arch has been removed. The east window is of two lights, without foil or tracery. On the south-east are two trefoil-headed lancets – on the south-west a lychnoscope with square head – at the north-east also a trefoil lancet. There is a piscina with trefoil head. The interior is dark and crowded. The font has a plain octagonal bowl on a stem of like form. In the churchyard is a fine yew tree. There are several gravestones to Roman Catholics.

This church was demolished in 1867, and rebuilt to the design of F.R. Kempson.

Cusop [97/35] S. Mary 9 September, 1851

A very small church in a lonely situation, two miles from the town of Hay. It consists of a nave and chancel, with a south porch of large size, in the upper part of which is hung the large single bell. From the want of a marked belfry, this church is not easily distinguished as such at a distance, though standing rather high and within an unusually large churchyard. On the south near the west end of the nave is a Norman small window – and also on the south side is a double lancet. At the west end is a square-headed slit. The chancel arch is plain and semicircular, on imposts. The east window is modern – on the north and south of the chancel are single lancets – the former closed. The font is cylindrical, covered with early kind of net or [?] lozenge work. There are steps from without on the east side of the porch leading to the belfry.

Clifford [97/34] S. Mary 9 September, 1851

This church derives its chief interest from its situation on a fine eminence commanding a very beautiful and extensive prospect. The church itself has been much modernised. It consists of a nave and chancel, with western tower: a large kind of transeptal excrescence added on the north in the Norman style in 1838 – at which time much alteration was made both within and without and the north wall for the most part rebuilt. The tower has rather a debased look of three stages, divided by string-courses, embattled but without buttresses. In the belfry story two obtuse-headed windows – in the other single ones, and there is the swelling base often seen in Welsh towers. The windows of the nave are modern. In the chancel are lancets on the south and on the north a Middle Pointed two-light window. The interior is pued and there is a barrel-organ. There are two slabs with cross florys, now lying outside the church, one near the north door, one on the slope of the churchyard gate – evidently dislodged in recent repairs. The churchyard is unusually spacious.

Glynne does not mention the rare superb oaken effigy of a priest, c.1300.

Yarpole [97/40] S. Leonard 27 August, 1852 and 1864

This church has a nave and chancel only, with south porch, but is chiefly remarkable for its odd detached belfry, of a rude but picturesque character, something savouring of the pigeon-house, and resembling that which occurs also at Pembridge, not far distant. This structure in its lower stage is of stone and quadrangular, lighted by plain slits – the low stone walls are covered by a tiled roof, on which rises a pointed wooden turret, having four small quatrefoil openings arranged in a horizontal line on the north and south. The internal arrangement presents very strong timber frame-work connected with the hanging of the three bells. This belfry stands at some distance from the body of the church on the south side. < *Drawing of the bell-tower.* 1864 Yarpole church recently restored by Scott with the addition of a north aisle. The whole reckoned successful.>

The chancel has been lately rebuilt in the Decorated style, with much pretension, but by no means successful. The east windows of three lights, the others of two. The interior is stalled, the sacrarium laid with tiles and on the south are two sedilia formed by an extension of the window-cill, divided by elbow(?) and a piscina rather more Early English and with trefoiled pedimented head and shafts – the basin circular. The nave has a poor roof, with tie-beams – the windows all deprived of tracery, but having hoods on corbels. There is a stone bracket in the jamb of a window.

The chancel arch is pointed, on octagonal shafts. The font is a good early one – the bowl octagonal and surrounded by a course of semicircular arches rising from shafts on low relief, the shafts having caps. and octagonal bases. Externally is a Decorated string-course under the wall-plate. The gables have crosses. The porch has trefoil-headed single windows in the sides. The outer door has octagonal shafts.

Glynne visited Yarpole twice, in 1852 and 1864. It seems that in 1852, the chancel had already been rebuilt, in a manner which Glynne deemed unsuccessful. In 1864 Sir George Gilbert Scott rebuilt the chancel and added the north aisle, and Glynne reckoned Scott's chancel 'successful'.

Richard's Castle [97/41] S. Bartholomew 27 August, 1852.

Here again we have a detached steeple, though very unlike the last [*Yarpole*]. The church is large and interesting, consisting of a wide nave with south aisle, a north transept or chapel, and a large chancel, a south porch to the nave. The roofs are rather high-pitched and separate. The tower stands at some distance to the east of the church, is low and plain, without much architectural detail – no buttresses, a belfry window of two lights without foils, and other openings mere slits. It stands adjacent to the churchyard wall, and formerly carried a spire – it may be of debased work built of older materials: the roof is pointed and of slate. The church is chiefly Decorated, but with some few indications of earlier work, especially on the north of the nave where there are Norman windows closed. At the west of the aisle is a double lancet. The west window of the nave is a good Perpendicular one of four lights. In the north chapel are some double lancets and one early Decorated (almost Early English) of this form [*diagram*]. The outer windows are all Decorated. In the north chapel, on the east and west, are square-headed ones of three lights, not quite similar – on the north of the same is a very odd one of four lights, each trefoil-headed, the two central ones lower than the others, and the upper part occupied by a circle containing a star of seven points. At the east end of the south aisle is a fine one of three lights, with ball-flowers on the outside of the mullions – over it is a quatrefoiled circle.

The arcade on the south of the nave has three very wide pointed arches with clustered piers, each of four octagonal shafts with moulded capitals containing the ball-flower ornament. Over the capital of each pier is a square pole [?]. There are two smaller pointed arches opening from the nave on the north of the chapel – the pier clustered, having [a] little battlemented capital, with a moulding containing square flowers. The chancel arch is wide and has similar shafts. Part of the rood screen is to be traced. In the south wall is a trefoiled piscina, with a squared ledge in which is the drain in form of a long slit, and adjacent to it is a square aumbrye.

The chancel is large, with plain open roof. Its windows all Decorated, the eastern of four lights, the others of two lights, that to the south-west square-headed. The sacrarium is wainscoted. There is a crypt under part of the chancel, lighted by a square opening with mullion. There are several fine pieces of stained glass in the windows, though mutilated. One in the south aisle has a fine green and yellow border – that at the east of the same head of Edw. I, and a fine border in the north chapel are heads of a king and queen: there is also some in the chancel. A pue near the chancel arch has a flat canopy over it. The priest's door has a hood at some distance above the arch. The south porch has a plain outer door and another within it. The font modern. The outer walls are for the most part stuccoed. The situation is picturesque and the view on the north side very grand. There is one sepulchral slab charged with a cross flory.

The old church at Richard's Castle is now in the care of the Churches' Conservation Trust, the present church one mile to the east being the creation of Norman Shaw in 1891 – 92.

Stretton Sugwas [97/50] 16 November, 1854

In arrangement this church resembles Credenhill – but the tower is wholly of wood-boards and having the pointed roof. The porch is also of wood. The windows on the south of the nave are square-headed, both Decorated and Perpendicular. Most of the windows are of the latter character, but there is a square-headed Decorated one on the north of the chancel. The chancel is long and there is a wood screen between it and the nave. On the south a priest's door.

The east end is ivied and the window closed. The church appears to have been repaired and is well cared for but rather inaccessible from being partly surrounded by the parsonage garden.

The church that Glynne saw was demolished, and the present church built on a new site, in 1878 – 81, the architect being a gentleman called Cheaike. Glynne does not mention the fine tympanum of Samson astride a lion, the work of the Herefordshire School.

Credenhill [97/49] S. Mary the Virgin 16 November, 1854

This church has only chancel and nave with western tower and south porch – but exhibits some features of interest. There is one lancet window on the north side of the nave and one window verging to Decorated and consisting of two trefoil-headed lights beneath a general arch, almost straight-sided and flattened – with a trefoiled circle between the heads. On the south of the nave the windows are all modern and bad.

The chancel arch is Early English – pointed, but low and small. On each side of it a fine niche with foliation of Decorated character – that on the south continued to the ground and having an oblique opening or hagioscope on its jamb. <The niche north of the chancel arch faces the west only. The other faces the east.> On the south side of the chancel are two lancet windows, trefoiled – and at the south-east a good early Decorated one of two trefoiled lights with trefoiled spherical triangle above them. On the north is also a two-light Decorated window. The east window is Decorated – of three lights. There is some ancient stained glass. The tower arch is small, pointed, and continuous. The font modern. The tower has base mouldings, but is much covered with ivy. It is surmounted by the pointed roof so common in Herefordshire. The roof is covered with strong flags. The porch is wholly of wood and a very good specimen – the front has fair feathering under the gable and a pointed arch forming the entrance, with fair moulding. The sides are with open panneling and the timbers within are arched.

'The ancient stained glass' in the south chancel window depicts superb portrayals of St. Thomas à Becket and St. Thomas Cantilupe. At some time after Glynne's visit, the arches to right and left of the chancel arch were constructed, replacing the niches and hagioscope which Glynne described.

Byford [97/51] S. John Baptist November 17th, 1854

A nice Early English church, having nave with south aisle, south transept, chancel, west tower and south porch, and all in nice order and apparently having undergone recent improvement. The south doorway very good and early in the style with excellent deep mouldings and shafts with capitals of foliage and a hood upon corbels of foliage. The arcade is of four arches, with circular columns having capitals of octagon form. The chancel arch pointed, and plain. The chancel has an east window of the common Herefordshire sort <sketch> – on the north one lancet – other windows about the church are of two simple trefoil-headed lights. The transept extends far east and has on its east side a large square-headed window of five lights simply trefoiled, but with trefoils above. <sketch> The porch has been rebuilt. The tower is Early English and small, with a doubtful battlement and belfry window, but having one string and single lancet windows in the lower part and no west door. The buttresses throughout are flat-faced. The font octagonal and plain. A lancet window at the west end of the aisle. The transept has a lofty gable and at its end a Perpendicular three-light window. The benches are open.

By 1854, Victorian restorations were getting under way, and this is the first time that Glynne comments, favourably, on recent changes. He will not always be so approving.

Mansel Gamage 97/52 November 17th, 1854

A small church, beautifully situated on a woody slope, but not very interesting, though characteristic of the locality.

It consists of a nave with south transept, chancel, western tower and south porch – the latter, following the local use, of wood, and a good specimen of that picturesque feature. The gable rudely feathered, the outer door arched – and above it the framework has a pierced quatrefoil. The sides open. There is a Herefordshire window, of the sort noted at Byford and elsewhere, in the transept – and some other windows on the south are of two lights trefoil-headed. Several windows in the chancel are modern, with wood mullions, containing stained glass and there are indications of well-meant alterations carried into effect too long ago and therefore unsatisfactory. The ground slopes considerably so that there is a steep ascent in the chancel towards the east. The chancel arch is pointed, and low – upon imposts. The tower is Perpendicular, embattled, with square turret at the north-west and much mantled with ivy. Against the north wall of the chancel is a fine ancient coffin-shaped slab, with a cross flory which has nailheads in the mouldings.

This church is now a private residence.

Bridge Sollers [97/51] S. Andrew 17 November, 1854

A small church having a nave with north aisle, chancel and west tower, with a south porch of wood. The features are Norman and Early English, the arcade of the nave has three semicircular arches of plain character; one column is circular, and one octagonal with [a] kind of cushion capitals. There is no chancel arch. The tower arch low and semicircular on imposts. There is one small Norman window, and in the north aisle some small trefoiled lancets and one double one of the same kind. The chancel has on the north two trefoil-headed lancets and on the south one of the double ones of the local character. The east window, another localism, of three lights like that at the east end of Byford. There is a semicircular plain doorway within the south porch, upon imposts. The tower is very small, and not unlike that of Byford and others in the county: without buttresses, with four tiers of little single windows and a modern battlement.

Glynne does not mention the carvings of dragons and a cat's head upon the imposts of the south doorway; these may be related to the Herefordshire School.

St. Peter in the City of Hereford
[97/31] 17 November, 1854

Originally an interesting church, strongly characteristic of the Herefordshire type – but sadly disfigured, both within and without. The outside especially suffering from mutilation and modern change, and the interior from frightful obstructions by pues and galleries in the most objectionable form.

The plan of the church is a nave with two aisles, a chancel with an aisle or chapel on the south, and a tower with good stone spire on the south side adjacent to the chancel. The nave and its aisles are wide, but the north aisle particularly so. The arcades are dissimilar – on each side with four pointed arches – those on the south of ordinary character, pointed with octagonal columns – those on the north curious from being acute *and straight*-sided, but with excellent mouldings – the piers clustered of four shafts <diagram> which have moulded capitals. This form of arch occurs elsewhere in the county of Hereford, especially in the north transept of the cathedral and its character appears to be Decorated. The east window of the north aisle is large and has five plain arched lights, within a containing arch. Most of the other windows are modern or mutilated, and nearly the whole of the south side, except the steeple, has been rebuilt. The situation is good and open on the south and west to a considerable square, so that if the exterior were restored the effect would be excellent.

The chancel is large – has on the north windows of three lights like that at the east of the aisle and a larger one at the east end. There is a small pointed arch between the chancel and its chapel, on circular columns, but now closed. The chancel has some fine stalls, with the canopies and decks in very good condition – the line of the canopies has a horizontal kind of overhanging fringe and the miseries remain. There is a marble pavement and modern Gothic altar and it would not be difficult to restore this fine spacious chancel to ecclesiastical propriety – but it is now entirely cut off from the nave by a large gallery containing the organ. There is also a double gallery at the west end of the nave. The arrangement of the small south chapel and the lower part of the steeple are difficult to make out from the darkness and the modern partitions which encumber them. The steeple itself is of good early Decorated work, having a plain moulded parapet without battlement and four corner pinnacles. The spire lofty and octagonal, with canopied windows. The belfry windows double – of rather uncommon style, having fine arch mouldings and trefoil feathering on each of two lights.

The exterior stone work is much decayed.

Since Glynne's visit, the south arcade has been rebuilt and now resembles the north arcade; and there have been sweeping changes to the interior.

Upper Sapey [97/65] S. Michael 20 April, 1855

A small church, as usual in the district, with only chancel and nave and south porch and modern stone belfry over the west end, chiefly of Norman character. The north doorway now closed <u>but windowed</u>, has a large fine arch of moulded orders with shafts, of which the capitals are sculptured in varied style. Within the porch is another doorway of the same style, having a good arch and shafts with well-sculptured capitals – the door itself with square head and tympanum over it, the arch concealed by the porch. The chancel arch is also good Norman with chevron mouldings and shafts, much resembling the doorways. There is also a Norman window on the north of the chancel and a Decorated one on the south. The east window has been closed up. There is a sepulchral arched recess on the south side of the nave: and on the same side a window of two trefoil-headed lights under a flat arch. The font has a cylindrical bowl with strong moulding round it, on an octagonal base and step.

In 1859 – 60, the chancel arch was transferred from its original position to the west end of the nave, so that it now acts as a tower arch.

Bodenham [97/73] S. Michael 27 October, 1857 [*probably an error for 1856*]

A large handsome church, cruciform in plan, with aisles to the nave and a large western tower. The chancel is much lower than the rest of the church and the transepts though equal in height to the nave, are short. The prevailing features are Decorated.

The interior in very good condition. The aisles have lean-to roofs but are almost equal in height to the nave – the arcade[s] on each side are tall, each of three good pointed arches on lofty octagonal pillars with capitals. A fourth arch somewhat similar on each side opens to the transept, but there is no lanthorn or crossing in the centre. There are also pointed arches springing straight from the wall between the transepts and aisles. There are no clerestory windows, though the string itself exists; the roof of the nave is new. There are ogee niches in the transepts. The chancel arch is a low pointed one, on octagonal pillars, and over it corresponding with the clerestory is a Decorated window of two lights. The arch to the tower is lofty and continuous. In the aisles are some two-light windows without foils – at the west [*end*] of the north aisle a three-light one of the Herefordshire kind of plain Decorated. At the end of the north transept is a three-light window [*diagram*] – that at the end of the south transept is of three lights not similar, but perhaps also Decorated. At the east side of this transept is one which seems to be Perpendicular. On the north side of the chancel arch the rood-door, communicating with the pulpit. In the north transept is a piscina.

The chancel has a Decorated east window of three lights – in its north wall under an arched sepulchral recess is a fine perfect effigy of a lady in a wimple, holding in her right hand on the shoulder of a child.

The north door, which is closed, has the ball-flower ornament – over the east gable of the clerestory is a bell-niche with a cross.

The tower is very large and appears to be late Perpendicular – three stages in height, with buttresses – moulded parapet and four panneled [?] square pinnacles at the corners. There is the lower part of an octagonal spire, which perhaps was never finished – having canopied spire lights. The belfry windows of two lights, without foils. The west doorway labeled – over it a two-light window. There is a south porch and a wooden lych-gate. Under the east window of the south transept is a very odd ogee slit-like opening, opening from the outside only. The pues all uniform. The font modern in the chancel. An organ in the tower. Two ugly high [*text unclear*] pulpits.

Wistaston [97/78] 27 October, 1856

A small chapel, within the parish of Marden. It seems to have been wholly rebuilt or at least nearly so in the seventeenth century, or even later. It is all of one space – with a small belfry over the west end. The walls are of good masonry – the windows in poor imitation of pointed tracery except the east window which is better and has three lights without tracery, and filled with stained glass in memory of some person, put in 1854.

The church was taken down in 1909.

Marden [97/71] S. Ethelbert 27 October, 1856

A fine church, with some curious and interesting features. The plan consists of a nave with north and south aisle, chancel with half-hexagonal apse, a north porch and a tower with handsome stone spire oddly situated adjoining the porch on the west side. The nave is Early English, the chancel Decorated. At the west end of the nave are two fine long lancets and a smaller one over them. At the west of the south aisle also a lancet – all of which are plain, but much splayed. There are also some lancets in the north aisle. The nave is lofty and has a clerestory. The arcade on each side is of four good tall Early English pointed arches with circular pillars which have circular capitals on the north and octagonal capitals on the south. The eastern responds are clustered with capital[s] of foliage. The clerestory has no existing windows. <In the south aisle are bad modern windows.> The nave has a cradle roof which as well as the lean-to roofs of the aisles is rather out of repair. The south aisle is wider than the northern. Across the north aisle a half-arch is carried, for the purpose of strength. The tower is set against the west bay of the north aisle but does not open by arches either to the aisle or porch. But there is a strong wall against the aisle with two ranges of stone corbels. The chancel arch is pointed and continuous. On its sides are traces of bolts – and on each side of it a recess or hagioscope, square towards the east and pointed towards the west and set oblique[ly]. The chancel has a poor modern ceiling. The chancel has numerous windows, three in the curious polygonal apse and

74

three on each side – all Decorated of two lights. <The chancel windows have star tracery.> There are two steps to the sacrarium. On the north side of the chancel is a plain priest's door. The east gable of the nave has a bell-niche. The font has an octagonal bowl with trefoil arches on each face and an octagonal stem. There are traces of painting on one of the northern columns of the nave. In the nave nice old open benches with linen pattern. A west gallery contains a barrel-organ.

The north porch has a cross on the apex of its gable – its inner doorway is continuous – and on its west side opens a good moulded door labeled, to the tower. The roof of the nave is of high pitch and slated.

The south porch is small – within it a good Early English doorway with continuous mouldings.

The steeple is a very pretty and uncommon composition and seems to be early Decorated. Its masonry is very fine – the tower of three stages with buttresses, moulded parapet and square pinnacles at the angles – a staircase at the north-east angle. The belfry windows of two lights – in the other stages a trefoil lancet in the second and a slit in the lowest. The spire octagonal, well-proportioned, but without ribs and within the tower. There is a very strong buttress in the north aisle. In the south aisle is a late brass to Henry Wallis – 1579. In the chancel a more curious one to Margaret wife of Sir Geo. Chute daughter of Wilfrid of Wistaston. There are two small figures of children, one in swaddling clothes. She died at 104 in 1662. <Pale death can scarcely find another So good a wife, so kind a mother, In all her actions so discreet As she that lies here at your feet.>

The irregular arrangement, with the fine steeple and roofs of varying height gives this church a very picturesque outline on every side. The river [Lugg] runs close to the churchyard, which is very large and a large portion to the west nearly untenanted by the dead. <St. Ethelbert is said to have [been] buried in Marden church [in] 806.>

Morton on Lugg [97/71] 27 October, 1856

A poor church having a nave with small south aisle and chancel, a north porch and mean low steeple at the west of the aisle – stuccoed with pointed tiled roof. At the west end of the nave is a trefoiled lancet. The tiled roof extends over both the nave and small aisle, which does not go quite to the west end. The arcade is very late Perpendicular- and consists of two very flat arches – with an octagonal pier having a capital. The windows are small and poor. At the east of the chancel is a Decorated one of two lights – and single lancets altered on the north and south. At the east of the aisle a rude trefoiled lancet. There is no division of chancel from the nave – but a screen encloses the east end of the aisle. The font is octagonal and plain. The porch is of wood and plaster, with some fair wood feathering.

The church was transformed – and very greatly improved – by the rebuilding of W.H. Knight in 1867. He retained the Perpendicular arcade, and the Perpendicular screen now encloses the organ. There are some excellent late Victorian mosaics in the chancel.

Pipe and Lyde [97/70] 27 October, 1856

A small church in rather a lonely site adjoining the turnpike road consisting of chancel and nave with low western tower having a dwarf spire. It seems of Early English origin, but has later portions. The tower is Early English, massive and short, without buttresses – with small lancet openings and a curious basement flagged and swelling outwards. The west window is odd – a lancet, with circle above it, beneath a hood with foliage corbels. The spire is short and shingled, and covers the square of the tower – much of the Sussex type – which is very much the general character of this church. On the north of the nave is a very small Norman window. On the south are some double trefoil-headed windows – one ogeed – of early Decorated character. The chancel arch does not exist. The east window is of the Hereford type of three lights – the centre not pointed and without tracery. Another window in the chancel is this [Y tracery; diagram] and then [one] on the south of the chancel is single and trefoil-headed. There [is] a stone staircase on the north of the chancel which led to the rood-loft, part of which remains – a fine horizontal cornice of foliage with vineleaf and grapes. The chancel roof is lower than that of the nave.

Some plain old open benches remain. The inner door of the south porch has good ancient iron-work

In the churchyard is the octagonal shaft of a cross.

The nave was rebuilt in the Early English style by F.R. Kempson in 1874, and he also added a broach spire to the tower.

77

Stoke Prior [97/75] S. - October 29th, 1856

This church has a long nave and chancel without aisles, a south porch and western tower surmounted by a curious heavy spire of shingles. The outer walls whitewashed, except the chancel which has lately been scraped and otherwise improved. There is a small Norman window on each side of the nave – that on the north has some stained glass. The only other windows of the nave are dormers in the roof. The chancel has some new lancets, but they are too wide. The east end has two – the others are single. There is no chancel arch, but a difference may be observed in the roofs. The roof of the nave has internally some Jacobean timbers. In the north wall of the nave is a square recess. In the chancel a small oblong piscina. The chancel is fitted with modern stalls – has a boarded roof and a harmonium. The nave is pued, and there are several modern monuments. The porch is of debased woodwork, yet not bad in effect, probably about 1600; having a bargeboard and feathering. Within it an obtuse-headed door. One of the dormer windows on the south is very large and seems to be coeval with the porch and the roof. The tower is very plain and massive – not rising much above the roof of the nave – it has only slits for openings and but few of them and no buttresses. The spire is marvellous in shape – the upper part having convex lines turning inward – and [*text unclear*] return the two portions. The font is octagonal and plain. The churchyard is very large and scarcely has any graves on the north side.

The church was rebuilt in 1863 by George Colley.

Humber [97/76] S. Mary 29 October, 1856

In form this church resembles the last named [*Stoke Prior*] almost exactly but here the length is less and the chancel rather better proportioned. The tower is almost exactly the same as at Stoke Prior – equally rude and massive – the spire is of the coarse shingled broach kind but has not the curved lines before noticed. The porch is of wood and very picturesque, though rude – the bargeboard has feathering and some pierced foiled openings above the horizontal timber which is just above the arch of entrance. There is no chancel arch. The nave is ceiled. The chancel has a new roof of wood and very good pitch, with open tracery and tie-beams. The chancel has been lately much improved and is fitted with stalls much like that of Stoke Prior. It has two lancets at the east end with circle above and a large stone bracket between them and splayed single lancets both north and south some of which are trefoiled. There is a piscina with multifoiled orifice. The windows of the nave are trefoiled lancets. The font seems to be new. There is a barrel-organ and a corona [*a circular chandelier*]. The situation is very pretty – on a woody bank and the churchyard is well-kept and rural.

The 'new' font described by Glynne has now been replaced by the original Norman font which was found in a neighbouring garden in the 1880s and reinstated in the church, but sadly disfigured (Marshall, 1949; Pevsner, 1963).

Pencombe [97/77] October 29th, 1856

A curious church though partially modernised. The plan includes a lofty nave without aisles, a chancel with eastern semicircular apse and a tower on the south side of the nave – also a wooden porch on the south. There are Norman features, and small windows of this style both on the north and south of the nave, set high in the wall. Most of the other windows of the nave are modern and bad – but at the west end is a rude two-light window which may be transitional to Decorated of this form [*sketch*] without hood. The nave is neat, but modernised in bad style and pewed, probably at the same time as the rebuilding of the tower which is recorded to have taken place in 1841. This is a poor imitation of Early English work but the original arch remains opening from it in the nave, which is semicircular, small and plain – springing from imposts. The chancel arch is similar – and merely a small opening surrounded by much wall. The chancel is remarkable from its two-fold division – the eastern part or apse being separated from the rest by a semicircular arch on imposts like the others. The windows of the apse vary and have been evidently altered – one is apparently original Norman, one is a lancet and one of two lights [*sketch*]. On the south is a triplet cinquefoiled. In the chancel window is some stained glass. The font has a plain octagonal bowl. There is a barrel-organ. The porch is as common in the county of wood. The roofs are tiled and high. The outline of the church is irregular – especially as seen from the north.

The church was rebuilt by Thomas Nicholson in 1864 – 65. He preserved the medieval arrangement of chancel and apse.

Cowarne Parva [97/80] S. - 29 October, 1856

A very small church on a steep bank, amidst much orchard scenery. It has no aisles, but three divisions in the roof – the roof flagged – and the walls mantled with ivy. There is no tower but an odd kind of humble belfry at the west end. There is a double lancet on the south side of the chancel, lately restored and having stained glass. <There is a stone partition between the chancel and nave. In the chancel a piscina.> Most of the other windows are bad and modern. On the north is a closed lancet. There is outwardly a second division to the nave. The chancel arch is plain and pointed . The font has an octagonal bowl on a stem. The porch is of wood.

Stone partitions between chancel and nave are rare. The church was rebuilt by F.R. Kempson in 1870.

Stoke Lacy [97/80] S. S. Peter and Paul October 29th, 1856

A small church, with only nave and chancel, a wooden plastered belfry over the west end and a south porch; situated within a churchyard of disproportionate size to the church. The chancel arch is Norman, on shafts – across it is a plain Perpendicular wooden screen. On the north of the nave are two very small Norman windows – some other windows are double lancets – and one Decorated, of two lights on the south. There is one small Norman window on the south of the nave, like that at Pipe. At the west end a single small lancet. The chancel has been rebuilt and has an eastern triplet. The font has an octagonal bowl. The porch is of woodwork and late date.

The church was rebuilt in 1863 by F.R. Kempson, retaining the original Norman chancel arch and the very good 16th-century screen.

Cowarne Magna [97/79] S. Mary 29 October, 1856

An interesting church situated on an abrupt eminence in a woody country – and consisting of a nave with south aisle, chancel, north vestry, western tower and south porch. The features are various. The tower is Early English – extremely massive – having a later battlement but with the original corbel-table. There are corner buttresses and large ones on the south and on the west side have been added for the purposes of strength. On the west side is one single lancet and on each side is an obtuse lancet in the lower story. The belfry windows have two lancet lights on a central octagonal shaft, contained within another arch. On the tower is an inscription of the sixteenth century. There was formerly a spire.

The interior is neat – the aisle is of equal height with the nave, without a separate roof and of good width. There is a good Decorated arcade of four arches, with light clustered piers of four shafts having moulded capitals. The chancel arch is pointed, upon octagonal shafts with square abaci. The east window of the aisle is Decorated, of three lights – another on the south is of two lights. The chancel has plain windows on each side of two lights without foliation and one with foliations restored. The east window is Perpendicular, of three lights of a local character. There is an ancient vestry on the north of the chancel, lighted by small slit openings. On the south of the altar is the recumbent effigy of a female in a ruff. There are traces of an arcade in the north wall, whence it appears there was once a north aisle – but a north doorway has an Early English look. In the chancel is a piscina.

The south porch is wood and plaster, mixed with stone and has a continuous outer doorway. The roofs have been covered with new slates. The font is modern. There are no graves on the north side.

There is a monumental figure in the south aisle.

St. Devereux [96/38] 1858 and 1867

This church has nave and chancel only, with western tower. On the north of the nave is one single and one double lancet: on the south is one lancet, and one fair Decorated window of two lights. The chancel arch is plain and pointed, springing from the wall without imposts. The chancel has on both north and south side square-headed Decorated windows of two lights, and at the east end a Perpendicular one of three lights. In the north wall are two sepulchral niches. The windows on the south side are of a kind of plate tracery. The seats are new and open. There is a small piscina in the chancel in shape of a spherical triangle.

The tower opens to the nave by a single pointed doorway. The tower is massive in its lower part – the upper story diminishing – it has no buttresses. On its west side is a single lancet – the other openings plain slits, except double belfry windows. The roof tiled and pointed.

Welsh Bicknor [97/85] 4 October, 1858

A small church close to the Wye, of which the whole of the body has recently been taken down and is being rebuilt. The tower remains untouched – is small and plain, standing at the west end of the south aisle has a pointed tiled roof – is without buttresses and has only slits for openings. The nave has a short south aisle stopped by the tower – the new arches have marble shafts in the pier, as has the chancel arch.

The whole of the church, including the tower, was expensively rebuilt in 1858, the architect being T.H. Rushforth of London.

Breinton [97/84] S. October 17th, 1858

A small church with only chancel and nave undivided and a south porch. Over the west end a wooden belfry. The walls of sandstone and appear to be Early English. The west doorway has the arch nearly semicircular and moulded. On the north are single trefoil lancets and one small Norman window. On the south a single ogee-trefoiled one. The east window a triplet, also trefoiled. On the north are early flat buttresses.

The church is in good order, has open seats and a small organ in the gallery. The roof plain and open. The font modern – no chancel arch,. The porch chiefly of wood.

There are some pretty gravestones in the churchyard, in the form of cross. The situation rural and secluded.

The church was rebuilt in 1866 – 70 by F.R. Kempson.

Holm Lacy [97/85] S. Cuthbert August, 1860

This church has nave, chancel, south aisle and north transept – south porch and west tower, principally of the local Decorated type. The chancel is not divided from the nave and the arcade is rather odd: four arches are narrow and pointed, but stilted, and with short square piers having no capitals – the fifth arch is wide and segmented but also without capitals. The arch to the transept is large and segmented on corbels. The chancel portion is divided from the south aisle or chapel by two narrow arches not uniform on a clustered pier of four shafts, transitional from Early English to Decorated. There is one lancet window in this south chapel and one in the south aisle of the nave; the other windows are varied. East and west of the aisle the windows are Decorated, of two lights – and on the south is one square-headed of two lights of the same date and some of two ogee-headed lights trefoiled. The east window of the chancel is Perpendicular, of three lights and contains some old stained glass. On the [*Glynne has omitted something here*] is a window of this local form [*sketch*] and another Decorated one in the chancel. In the chancel is a piscina which looks Early English of this form [*sketch*] and near to it a bracket. In the south chapel the cill of a window is prolonged in the centre rather curiously, so as to form a sedile – there is also a piscina of trefoil form, having an octofoil orifice. In the chapel is a fine marble tomb AD 1716 to some of the Scudamore family, also an altar tomb, with alabaster figures of knight and lady, with blasoned heraldic shields to John Scudamore 1550. The east window of this chapel has new memorial glass. The tower arch is very small, more like a door. The font is a modern one of marble. The interior is neat and carefully kept, but somewhat bare. There is a barrel-organ in a gallery. The tower has a moulded parapet and corner buttresses – is rather low and appears to be Perpendicular. The belfry windows of two lights and on the west a long slit. It has eight bells. The south porch has a doorway with continuous mouldings. The exterior is of picturesque grey stone and the lovely situation near the parsonage is pretty – not far from the Wye but buried in trees. In the churchyard is the shaft of a cross and the tomb of Lady Scudamore (ob[ii]t 1859) with cross on the slab.

Tedstone Delamere [97/87] S. James 13 September, 1860

Another very small church having chancel and nave with wooden bell-cot and small spire over the west end and a new south porch of timber. The whole has been recently effectually restored by G.G. Scott, and many of the windows and part of the walls are new. The site is very beautiful amidst lovely scenery, secluded and abounding in hill and wood. The nave is of Norman origin – the chancel Early English but entirely rebuilt. On the south of the nave is one early Norman window and one with flattened trefoil head – and there are very small original Norman windows both north and south. The chancel arch has continuous mouldings and is pointed. There is a wood rood screen. The east window has three unequal lancets, with marble shafts – all under a large arch and circles in the space above the lancets. It is filled with stained glass. The seats are open – the pulpit of stone with marble shafts, the reredos of glazed tiles. The old font is in the churchyard – the new one has a square bowl with foliated circles and four marble shafts. There is an organ – two old slabs charged with crosses. The belfry turret rests on timbers set on the ground. The whole is satisfactory and pleasing.

As the 1860s proceed, Glynne encounters increasing numbers of churches which have been restored, some of which, as here, he approves.

Whitbourne [97/88] S. John Baptist September 13th, 1860

A larger church than the last [*Tedstone Delamere and Shelsley Parva, Worcestershire*], but which has not like them had the advantage of recent restoration and improvement. It has however no aisles – has merely a nave and chancel, which have no architectural distinction, north porch, vestry north of the chancel and western tower.

There are Norman features on the south, a fair doorway with chevron mouldings and one order of shafts – also one Norman window and one lancet south of the chancel. South of the nave is a trefoil lancet much splayed and one set low in the wall: also a square-headed Perpendicular window of three lights. The chancel has on the north a trefoil lancet – at the east a four-light Perpendicular window.

The interior is ugly and villainously pued. On the north of the chancel is an obituary window of new stained glass. The roof of the chancel is coved, with ribs. There is no chancel arch – but a deep west gallery. Over the entrance to the chancel is a modern glazed turret containing the Sancti bell. The font is early, of cylindrical form. The tower arch is pointed, springing at once from the walls. The tower Perpendicular, embattled with four pinnacles and corner buttresses. The west window of three lights, the belfry windows of two lights. The north porch has an odd projecting story and a large board of foliage.

There is a lich gate.

A north aisle was added in 1866, by A.E. Perkins.

Llandinabo [97/91] S. Dinabo September 13th, 1861

A small church scarcely worthy of notice, having apparently been wholly rebuilt. It has a nave and chancel only, with a wooden belfry over the west end. The whole is poor meagre Gothic – the only part that may be original is the east window which is in the local Herefordshire type and maybe re-inserted. The churchyard is large.

The church was again rebuilt in 1881 by A. Lloyd Oswell, who encased the outer walls of the previous building described by Glynne; it now contains a notable late medieval rood-screen, one of the best in the county. It is strange that Glynne did not record it – was it present in the church in 1861?

Lanwarne [90/3] S. John September 13th , 1861

This church has a nave and chancel with south aisle and north transept, a western tower and a south porch. Its general arrangement much resembles Hentland and Holm Lacy <and Sellack, as originally it was>. There is no chancel arch, a peculiarity not uncommon in Herefordshire. The roofs are tiled. There are three good Decorated. windows in the south aisle of the nave, of two lights, and another at the east end of the same. The transept has a lancet on the east side and other windows on the north have two lights without tracery or foliation.

The arcade of the nave has obtusely pointed arches on circular columns. The transept opens to the nave by a pointed arch. The chancel has on the south Decorated windows of two lights with rather peculiar tracery verging to Perpendicular. The east window is of two lights and mutilated. The font is small and modern. There is only a doorway arch from the nave to the tower. The tower is Perpendicular and strongly built, embattled, with a square turret at the north-east rising above the parapet. The interior of the church is rather dark.

Three years after Glynne's visit, the church was abandoned because of repeated trouble with the foundations; its picturesque roofless ruins survive. A new church was built a short distance to the west.

Pencoyd [90/2] S. Denis 13 September, 1861

This church is somewhat forlorn and neglected – consists of a nave and chancel with western tower. There is no architectural division whatever between nave and chancel – the roof has tie-beams, the fittings mean and decaying. There is one obtuse-headed lancet on the south, and one square-headed window of two lights which seems to be Decorated. The east window is Decorated of two lights. There is also a single ogee-headed one on the south, and some fragments of ancient stained glass may be seen. There is a plain mutilated wood screen of Perpendicular character between the nave and chancel. The font is a circular cup. The tower opens to the nave by a small pointed doorway. The tower is very small and plain, without string nor buttress, with lancet belfry window and other slit-like openings. The parapet is plain and not embattled. There is a south porch of wood.

The church was restored and the chancel rebuilt in 1877 – 78.

Tretire [90/2] S. Mary 13 September, 1861

This church has been wholly rebuilt from the plans of Wyatt and is a creditable small church, with simple Decorated windows and properly fitted with open benches.

The church was rebuilt in 1856; the illustration is of the old church.

Welsh Newton church

Welsh Newton [90/1] S. Mary 13 September, 1861

This church has a nave and chancel without aisles, a south porch and a curious small quasi-steeple with short spire at the west end.

The windows on the north of the nave are double lancets. Most of the others are wide single ones both in nave and chancel and above them externally runs a horizontal cornice with rude corbels. On the south of the nave is a gabled dormer window formed in the roof, which is Decorated of two lights. The east window of the chancel is Early English transitional to Decorated of two lights, with circle above, under a pointed hood on corbels. <The east window has flowered mouldings internally.> The south-west window of the chancel has the cill prolonged for a window seat, and there is a trefoil-headed niche in the south-east angle of the chancel.

The most curious feature in the church is the triple arcade which divides the nave from the chancel. The three arches are pointed with fair mouldings with octagonal piers having ball-flower in the outer mouldings. Above is a horizontal moulding, also filled with the ball-flower. The bay windows seem to have been connected with the rood-loft.

The font has a circular cup-shaped bowl. At the west end of the nave are two lancets, between which is placed the little shallow steeple, which seems to be a debased addition, has plain slit opening and crowned by a diminutive stone spire containing two bells. <The two western lancets are much splayed.>

The nave has a coved roof, with ribs and bosses. The chancel roof is similar. There are some rude open benches with [some] kind of knobs at the ends. The situation is beautiful and rural, the ground of the churchyard very uneven and the surrounding scenery sylvan and lovely.

It is perhaps not surprising that Glynne does not mention the grave in the churchyard of St. John Kemble; he was a Catholic priest who served in Monmouthshire and Herefordshire for 53 years. After the scare of the Titus Oates plot in 1678, he was apprehended at the age of 80 years, and hanged, drawn and quartered at Hereford.

Whitchurch [97/22] S. Dubricius 13 September, 1861

This church has lately been in a great measure reconstructed and a north aisle added to the nave. The chancel arch is original, rather an awkwardly shaped pointed one, with continuous mouldings and no capitals. The chancel is perhaps altogether original, has Decorated window on the east of three lights, on the north of two lights and a poor one on the south. On the north a vestry has been added. The new arcade of the nave has three pointed arches with octagonal pillars having capitals. The north windows are of course new and Decorated of two and three lights. The west end has two lancets trefoiled and above the heads in the centre a quatrefoiled circle. Over the gable has been added a pointed bell-cot with two open arches for bells. Some of the original windows have been re-inserted in the new south wall – one Perpendicular of four lights, subarcuated, and another rather singular consisting of two arched compartments each of two lights, and a circle above in the centre [*sketch*]. The interior is neat and fitted up with propriety having new open benches. The font is Norman – a circular bowl sculpted with a Norman arcade. There is a south porch. In the churchyard the high shaft of a cross on a niched base. The site is very pretty, on elevated ground close to the Wye.

Glynne is now in Archenfield, the part of Herefordshire where Welsh influence is strong, and where dedications to obscure Welsh saints are frequent – note St. Dubricius here and at Hentland, and St. Tysilio at Sellack.

Sellack [97/89] S. Tesiliah [sic] 14 September, 1861

This church has rather a singular appearance both from its curiously constructed original spire steeple and the modern alterations which have taken place in the body: but the situation is retired and beautiful. It consists of a nave which had a north aisle now in great measure absorbed by an ugly modern extension of a quasi-transept, a chancel with north aisle, western tower with spire and south porch. The material is old red sandstone. The tower is rather small and not rising

much above the roof of the nave – is without buttresses but with spreading base mouldings – lighted only by a few small slits and surmounted by a stone broach spire which is much higher than the tower and is ribbed at the angles and has four canopied spire lights on the cardinal sides. The porch is large, has open side windows of two lights – the outer doorway with continuous arch mouldings – the inner doorway somewhat similar and over it a cinquefoiled niche. There is a stoup within the porch. The south side of the church externally has been changed from its original character by the formation of two gabled bays in which windows are inserted, but which seem to be original ones pushed up. One of three lights, Decorated of a local kind <diagram>, the other of two lights also Decorated – below these are square-headed Decorated, small windows of two lights. The west of the north aisle is of similar character of three lights. The aisle was originally very narrow, but the effect is greatly injured by the ugly extension of the transept. There remains one arch of the Norman arcade next the west end with large circular columns. There is no chancel arch, rather according to local custom as at Hentland, Lanwarne, Holm Lacy etc. The chancel has a short aisle on the north, opening to it by one plain pointed arch on imposts. The east window Perpendicular – of four lights subarcuated – on the north is one three-light window like that west of the aisle – and on the south are two plain square-headed windows also Decorated, of two lights. The font is a plain octagon. There is a vestry north of the chancel. In the churchyard, on the south side, is the shaft of a cross with high base charged with niches.

Hentland [97/90] S. Dubricius 14 September, 1861

This church now put into nice order is in a retired situation amidst shady trees and orchards. The plan is nave with north aisle, chancel, west tower and north porch. The general arrangement is like that of Sellack, but the public entrance is on the north side. The south wall has been renovated and has Decorated windows of two lights with square heads – one of two lights of this form [*diagram*] and one single with trefoil head.

The nave has an arcade of four rather acute pointed arches, with small curvature, on low octagonal pillars with capitals. <The piers of the arcade are of party coloured horizontal courses.> There is no chancel arch but a late wood screen dividing the chancel. <There is a good ascent to the altar.> The roof is a new one coved and ribbed. The windows of the north aisle are all renovated which are lancets with trefoil heads. The chancel has two lancets with trefoil heads on each side. The east window is of a common Herefordshire type of three lights, without tracery – the central one not arched. The chancel is fitted with stalls having poppy ends and laid with fine glazed tiles. The nave has open seats of pine. The font is a plain octagon. The porch is new. The tower arch is open and springs straight from the wall. The tower is Decorated – embattled with corner buttresses and a square turret at the north-east. <The tower is of very good colour.> It has base mouldings, belfry windows of two lights with string below – on the west a Perpendicular three-light window but no door.

In the churchyard on the north is a good cross – the upper part complete and gabled with four sculptured faces having niches containing bas reliefs of the Crucifixion and Saints. There is a fine yew tree on the same side, formed into a seat.

It is said that St. Dubricius founded a monastic site here in the 6th century

Aston [90/11] S. Giles 14 June, 1862

An extremely small church but consisting of nave and chancel divided by a continuous pointed arch. The nave is Norman – has one very small narrow window of that style on the north – and a curious doorway also on the north, remarkable to be found in so small and obscure a church. The outer moulding richly chevroned, there are no shafts, but richly sculptured impost mouldings of which the east displays two courses of foliage – the other seems to represent serpents in both courses. The tympanum has in the centre the Holy Lamb within a circular medallion, and on each side are winged animals. The outer order of the tympanum displays four animals like hares or weasels with foliage in the centre. Under the tympanum and just above the door-case is a billet cornice [*billet is a kind of moulding*]. The south doorway is also Norman, with tympanum, but is quite plain. On the south is a modern window. The chancel has undergone some restoration – has at the east a trefoil-headed lancet – and a double one on the south. The seats are open. The font is a makeshift small bowl on wooden stem.

The tympanum is now recognised as an early work of the Herefordshire School of Romanesque Sculpture.

Kingstone [90/36] S. Michael 18 May, 1864

A neat church consisting of nave with south aisle, chancel with south aisle, south porch and tower at the west of the nave. The condition is good and partial renovation has taken place. The nave has an Early English arcade of three pointed arches, with large cylindrical pillars with indented capitals. There are two Early English arches between the chancel and its aisle, having [a] circular pillar smaller than those in the nave and [a] capital of foliage. <There is a similar arch to both chancels, if they may be so called, rising from the adjacent pillar of the arcade. The altar is placed at the east end of the southern.> The chancel arch is pointed, upon cylindrical shafts rising at once from the capitals without further division of wall, the arcade running continuously from east to west. There are some two-light Decorated windows north of the nave restored. The windows on the south are of the same date, and renovated. One is single with obtuse trefoil head, another of two trefoil-headed lights beneath a pointed head, with stone in the interval on which is a kind of dial-like figure [dial -? some kind of mass-dial]. <The chancel is lower than the nave.> In the chancel are some narrow lancets and an east window Decorated of two lights. The organ is in the northern chancel. There is a three-light window at the west of three lights with ungraceful Flamboyant tracery. The interior is lofty and of good effect and the seats all open. The tower arch is pointed and the tower looks new, of fresh stonework, embattled, with eight rather crowded pinnacles and a belfry window Decorated of two lights. <During Whitsun week, this church was prettily decorated with evergreens.> The porch is a new one of wood. The walls mostly of red stone. The roofs covered with stone flags. The churchyard very pretty. <In the churchyard on the south is the base of a cross.> The west door has continuous arch mouldings. The south doorway has semicircular head, on imposts.

Dorston [90/44] S. Peter 18 May, 1864

This church has hardly a vestige of ancient work, though it is possible that some of the walls may be. At any rate the original plan seems to be preserved, viz. a chancel and nave without aisles, with western tower and south porch. In the chancel some windows may be original Perpendicular, of two lights, all the others are of debased character. On the north of the altar is a small arched recess. The tower is plain and embattled, but wholly devoid of character and the font is plain. The chancel is long and there is no chancel arch.

The medieval church apart from the tower (which survives) was demolished in 1827, when the church visited by Glynne was built. This in turn was demolished in 1889, when the present church was built to the design of Messrs. Nicholson and Son.

Turnastone [90/42] S. Mary 18 May, 1864

A small church, somewhat neglected, having only nave and chancel undistinguished with a small wooden belfry over the west end. The south doorway has a round arch on shafts and looks transitional from Norman. The south porch is a picturesque one of wood. There has been very little alteration carried on. The windows on the north and south are single trefoil-headed lancets. The east window has however been destroyed and replaced by a very mean one. The north doorway is closed. The roof is wholly coved with ribs and bosses of foliage. The only distinction of chancel is marked by a tie-beam in the roof. On the south of the chancel is a priest's door. There is also a piscina with trefoil-headed arch and two stone brackets in the east wall. The pulpit is a small plain old one of wood. The font is a plain circular bowl.

Within the sacrarium is a slab with incised figures, well-preserved, of a knight and lady and an inscription which might be easily deciphered if a little time could be given. "Hic jacent corpora Roberti [*blank*] Armig. et Agnetis uxoris eius" – and "AD 1529". The interior is dreary, containing a few old pues.

Vowchurch [90/43] S. Bartholomew 18 May, 1864

This church has a nave and chancel, in one space, of considerable length and fair height, with a south porch and a plastered bell-cot over the west end, which rests upon timbers set on the ground within the church. The west window may perhaps be Norman, but the head is cut. On the south of the nave is one decidedly Norman window, set high up near the porch, and two windows of two lights trefoiled, not included under a large arch. On the north is one single trefoil-headed window and one Decorated of two lights. The east window is of the Hereford sort, of three lights, the central one not arched. The south and north doorways have continuous mouldings.

The interior has a fine effect and is in good order. The roof and the screen are apparently of Elizabethan work and good of the kind. The roof is high-pitched – the tie-beams on carved brackets and open timber-work above the tie-beams – and the whole supported on octagonal longitudinal pillars of wood detached from the walls of the church and thus showing that this roof was a later addition. There are painted armorial shields on the nave roof and that in the chancel is coloured blue with stars. The screen is also remarkable as having been erected after the Reformation to separate the chancel and is of similar character to the roof with blazoned armorial shields. The chancel is large and shallow, with woodwork somewhat similar. There is a double piscina and shelf under a pointed arch on the south of the chancel – and in the south wall of the nave near the screen is a square recess. In the north wall are two sepulchral arched recesses under the windows. The font has a circular bowl, having an ornament which is of doubtful character, on a renewed circular stem. In the chancel is a harmonium.

There is a kind of stone seat or ledge externally on the south side, and the porch is a pretty one of wood, with open timbers not unlike that at Turnastone. In the churchyard on the south is the base of a cross.

The screen is dated 1613, and behind it is a board inscribed, 'Heare below ly the body of Thomas Hill ande Marget his wife, whose children made this skryne.' The roof is of approximately the same date.

Ewias Harold [90/37] S. Michael 19 May, 1864

A curious church of some length and rather wide, but comprising only nave and chancel without aisles, with a south porch and large low western tower. The latter is rather singular in character, of Early English work covered with a pointed tiled roof. There is a large projecting structure with penthouse top at the south-west angle, having slit-like openings. There are no buttresses, and the south side has the only enrichment – and what is singular on the south, a doorway with two bold orders, the inner carried on huge circular shafts with capitals. Over this door is a window of two lancets beneath an arch with lozenge in the head. Over this is a single lancet, and higher up a belfry window of three lancets under an obtuse arch having two orders of shafts; below this window is a string. The tower spreads out towards the base. On the other three sides it is very plain and has no windows except those of the belfry on the north and east, which are of two lights under an arch. The west wall is completely dead. To the nave the tower opens only by a doorway.

The windows of the nave are unhappily poor modern Gothic. <One window north of the nave seems to be Early English – has two lights with a lozenge between their heads.> In the chancel on the south are two single lancets, and none at all on the north. The east window of two lights, of doubtful character. The chancel arch is flat and of doubtful character. The interior very neat, but bare with whitewashed walls, but partially cleared in the chancel. The chancel is stalled in a Jacobean fashion, the seats, all open and the pulpit and desk are of the same style. The sacrarium is large and wainscoted, evidently coeval with the seats etc. There is a good Decorated tomb on the north side of the altar. The canopy is recessed in the wall and has good double feathering with clustered shafts having moulded capitals. The effigy is of a lady in a wimple holding in her hands a kind of circular box. The roofs are plain, with tie-beams. The porch bad. The west gallery has some screenwork which may have belonged to the rood-loft. The font has an octagonal bowl with sunk panneling, on a circular stem. <The churchyard is wholly to the south: beautifully decked with flowers and evergreens.>

The nave was rebuilt in 1868. It is now recognised that the effigy of the lady with a wimple holds her heart in her hands.

Dulas [90/38] St. Michael 19 May, 1864

A small church with only chancel and nave, having a wooden bell-cot over the west end. The walls are whitewashed. The east window is a plain double lancet, and north and south of the chancel are two lancets. The nave has no windows on the north, and one on the south is square-headed. The west doorway is semi-Norman – the outer arch is semicircular and has a cylindrical moulding on shafts with capitals of odd sculpture. The door arch is pointed. Above is a new window inserted. The south doorway is modern. There is no chancel arch and the roof is simply coved, with tie-beams. The interior is rude, but the pews have been removed and replaced by chairs. On the south of the chancel is a plain piscina. The reredos is evidently a recent introduction and has good wood-carving. Beneath the east window outwardly runs a rude stone projecting ledge or seat. In the churchyard is the shaft of a cross on steps.

This church was demolished in 1865, and a new building in the Early English style was erected to the design of G.C. Haddon.

Brampton Brian [97/75] S. Barnabas 18 July, 1864 (and Oct. 1824)

This church was almost wholly rebuilt in 1650 having been destroyed in the parliamentary wars in 1643. It is only interesting as showing how churches were built at that time. It is probable that some portion of the ancient walls, especially at the south-west, remain and in the south wall, near the east end, is the effigy of a lady under an arch holding in her hand what looks like a heart, much hid by a pue.

The church is wide and lofty, but has no distinction of chancel. The roof is striking, open and with hammer-beams – the windows are all square-headed and without mullions, save a three-light Decorated one at the east end, lately inserted and filled with stained glass. A new bell-turret has been added on the south side, and the walls are prettily mantled with ivy.

In 1643, the church was held by the Royalists, while Brampton Bryan castle was held for Parliament by Lady Brilliana Harley.

Canon Pyon [90/19] S. Laurence 11 September, 1865

This church has nave with north and south aisles, chancel with north aisle, and tower at the south side of the nave forming a porch in its lower story. The south aisle of the nave is very narrow. The nave has Early English arcades – on each side four pointed arches on circular columns with moulded capitals somewhat varied, but mutilated. There is a clerestory with plain square small windows, of late date, on the south but not on the north. The narrow south aisle has a lean-to roof and stone arches are carried across it from the piers. The church was undergoing a restoration, the piers entirely removed and the roof under repair. There is a trefoil-headed niche with piscina in the south aisle. The windows have mostly a transitional character from Early English to Decorated. That at the west of the nave has four trefoil lights under a general arch – at the west of the north aisle it is of three similar lights. That at west of the south aisle is a trefoil-headed lancet. Several windows of the nave are bad, and some Perpendicular and mutilated, in the roof dormer windows have been inserted. The north aisle is of good width and has a separate roof of good pitch.

There is no chancel arch and the chancel roof is new. Between the chancel and north aisle is one Early English arch. This aisle has a ball-flower cornice and various windows – one trefoil-headed lancet – one with a kind of plate tracery, with two trefoil-headed lights with quatrefoil above – and included in a pointed arch with hood. At the east end is one of the peculiar Herefordshire windows of three lights, which has a shouldered rear arch – the centre light not arched. In this aisle is a trefoil-headed piscina with quatrefoil orifice.

The chancel has on the south side a plain two-light window. The east window is Perpendicular, of three lights, and has some fragments of old stained glass. <*sketch.* There is a single-light window in the gable over the east window of the north aisle.> In the chancel are some stone brackets, portions of the old stalls, also some Perpendicular wood screen-work. On the south is a piscina with trefoiled niche and projecting basin upon a head corbel. The sacrarium has lately been laid with ornamental tiles.

There is an ancient vestry at the east of the north aisle which has a lancet on the east side, having a lean-to roof. The font has an octagonal bowl, the upper part having a course of quatrefoil panneling of Perpendicular character – the lower part however seems to be Early English.

The material of which this church is built is the old red sandstone. The chancel has been partially rebuilt. The tower is massive – has an embattled parapet and two string courses and corner buttresses. The belfry window appears to be Decorated, of two lights, and in the stage below is a single light. The outer doorway forming the entrance to the church has a large continuous arch.

The churchyard is unusually spacious.

Kings Pyon [90/17] S. Mary 11 September, 1865

This church has nave, south transept and chancel, with south porch and western tower situated on an elevated tump in the midst of the village. The roofs are of good pitch and covered with stone flags, that of the chancel being lower than that of the nave. The tower is of the plain rude kind found often in Wales, without buttress, and having the swelling base, and a plain battlement. On the west side a single trefoil-headed lancet. On the east a double lancet. It is much covered with ivy and opens to the nave by a low doorway only. The porch is of wood. <The porch is modern.> Within it a Norman doorway with cylindrical moulding and shafts. The nave roof is open and lofty, and a very fair specimen with tie-beams and trefoiled framework. The transept is more of the nature of a chapel and opens to the nave by two narrow pointed arches, with central circular column having octagonal capital and responds, one clustered, the other circular. The roof of the transept is open and has some trefoil cusping. This transept is of Decorated character and has evidently been a chantry chapel. The east window is of three lights trefoiled, under a pointed arch; its southern window of three lights with square head and shouldered chamfered rear arch and a kind of reticulated tracery <*sketch*>. Beneath it is a fine sepulchre of corresponding date – the tomb panneled, under a canopy which has hanging double feathering with fleur de lys at the points and in the spandrels quatrefoiled circles – above, a horizontal cornice of ball-flower. The effigies of a knight and lady remain. <The knight has a chain corslet, but much mutilated. The lady has a head-dress.> In this chapel is also a piscina with trefoil-headed niche. On its west side is a large stair-turret. There are two bad windows on the north of the nave – also one Norman window and a doorway of plain Norman character, with cylindrical moulding and hood. On the south of the nave are square-headed windows of three lights.

The chancel arch is Early English with two plain orders and clustered shafts of two orders, with flowered caps and abaci on the west side. The chancel has on the north one small Norman window and one lancet. The east window Decorated of two lights, with string under it and on the south a priest's door of multifoiled (or cinquefoiled) form with mouldings, but no hood <*sketch*>. On the north side of the chancel is a large vestry with chamber over it, and gable. Lighted by single light windows, one in the gable which is bounded by a string-course <*sketch*>. In the chancel is a Scudamore organ – but the chancel is rather blocked up. The font has a circular cup-shaped bowl.

Stretford [90/16] S. Peter 11 September, 1865

A small church in a secluded situation having nave and chancel with north aisle, south porch and a pointed wooden belfry over the west end. On the north are two closed small windows, one Norman, one EE. The east and west gables are both, rather uncommonly, carried to one point over both aisles, so as to give no indication outwardly of the existence of an aisle. On the west front appears two windows, each of two ogee trefoiled lights, a local type and a moulded circle above the northern of them. The east end has two windows, of debased character, one of two lights and one of three – this end is finely mantled with ivy. On the south side are two single lancet windows, not of the same size. On the north are no windows open. The nave has two plain EE arches dividing the aisle, on a circular column. The chancel has one pointed arch to the aisle, on the east, upon a shaft with ball-flowered mouldings in the capital, on the west on a circular shaft. The east end of the chancel has a panneled roof: there is a plain Perpendicular rood screen at the entrance of the chancel. In the north aisle of the chancel a feathered sepulchral arch in the wall. The porch is of wood framework, of late character and picturesque. The church is not in good order, but its situation shaded by old trees is pretty and retired.

Stretford church is now in the care of the Churches Conservation Trust.

Monkland

This church has been lately partially rebuilt, and has undergone a complete and very satisfactory restoration in true ecclesiastical spirit.

It consists of a nave and chancel only, with western tower and porch. The whole of the original features that could be traced, seem to have been reproduced and the old red sandstone is left bare in the interior. The windows of the nave are irregularly set. On each side are two small Norman ones. On the north also one lancet and one Decorated of two lights. On the south are two Decorated ones. The tower arch is a wide pointed one on octagonal shafts and of course open to the nave. The chancel arch is a lofty pointed one on octagonal shafts. The nave has an open roof with ribs – that of the chancel is coved and panneled [*word unclear*]. An addition has been made on the north of the chancel for an organ chamber. The chancel has a Decorated east window of three lights and on the south two sedilia with trefoil heads and a double piscina. There is a new sculptured reredos and stalls in the chancel. The fittings are all new and of oak. In the nave open benches and a good pulpit. The font has a bowl of circular cup-shape. The porch is a new one of timber.

The tower is massive, of the local type – has buttresses and lancet belfry windows – and a west window of a trefoil-headed lancet. The tower has no parapet, but is terminated by a pointed wood roof.

The 'very satisfactory restoration in true ecclesiastical spirit' was the work of the eminent High-church Victorian architect, G.E. Street (1824 – 81), who faithfully reproduced the design of the original church. The interior is Victorian art of the highest order. With this enthusiastic endorsement, Glynne betrays his sympathy with the aims of the Ecclesiological movement, which sought to bring back High-Church ritual in the Church of England.

Much Dewchurch [90/48] S. David April, 1858 and 1 August, 1867

This church has a chancel and nave, with western tower, of good height and proportions, recently restored and partially reconstructed. The tower is very massive and without buttresses and surmounted by a pointed shingled roof which has [a] sort of spire lights and rises high. There is a single lancet both on the north and south and west and on the west a doorway with continuous arch mouldings apparently Decorated. The south doorway within the porch is Norman, with square door-head and tympanum above, but no sculpture or mouldings. On the south side of the nave near the west end is a small narrow Norman window and there is a similar one on the north. Some other windows of the nave are Decorated of two lights and one a single lancet trefoliated in the head. The chancel has Decorated two-light windows on the south. The east window Perpendicular of three lights. Many of the windows have new coloured glass and the churchyard is very pretty. On the south side is the shaft of a cross.

Hatfield [90/24] S. Leonard 12 August, 1867

A small church, consisting of nave and chancel only, with a western porch and wooden belfry over the north end. The porch is of wood, with open framework. The nave is rather long in proportion to its width and the chancel arch is obtusely pointed, springing from the wall without imposts. The east end has two plain lancets, filled with coloured glass. The other windows are mostly Perpendicular square-headed of two lights, but on the north side of the chancel is a very small Norman one, a feature not uncommon in these parts. The font seems to be new – an octagonal bowl on clustered shafts.

Glynne does not mention the herringbone masonry and the tufa stone, features which indicate that Hatfield is an early Norman building, probably late 11ᵗʰ century.

Puddlestone [90/25] S. Peter 12 August, 1867

This church has been mainly reconstructed and the whole of the walls are said to be new – but so well done as to have the effect of being original.

The plan is a clerestoried nave with aisles, chancel with vestry and organ-chamber on the north, south porch and western tower with shingled spire. The walls are of old red sandstone and the Herefordshire character of which is well maintained throughout – the interior being richly arranged for high ritual. The nave is wide but short, and the aisles narrow – the roofs are open and wholly new. The arcades of the nave have on each side three Early English arches, upon circular columns, with round moulded capitals. The clerestory has small single lancets set over the piers, and the roof of the same is sloping and covered with tiles. There is no chancel arch. The windows of the aisles vary – some of two lights with quatrefoil above – some of two trefoil lights, over which is a small circle. The south porch is new – the doorway within it has continuous mouldings.

The tower is low and Early English – opens to the nave by a low obtuse arch over which is a lancet. It has also single lancets north and south – the belfry windows plain double lancets – the spire shingled and small. On the west side is a Norman doorway, having two orders of moulding on imposts and no shafts. The inner moulding plain – the outer has chevron ornament. In the tympanum is sculptured some sort of rude foliage of a character varying from Norman to Early English.

The nave is fitted with open seats. Between the nave and chancel is a wood screen and rood-loft, with a new rood.

The chancel is rather sumptuous in its fittings. It has on the south two single lancets – and one window of two trefoiled lights, the cill formed into a sedile, near which is a piscina with pedimental canopy crocketed and finialed. The east window is Geometrical, of three lights, having marble shafts in the jambs and filled with fine new coloured glass. The reredos is of stone and has rich sculpture in medallions – in the centre, the Man of Sorrows. The sacrarium is laid with fine tiles. The chancel is stalled and the roof is coved and panneled, and enriched with some rather odd tracery. There is a sepulchral arch on the north of the chancel, over which is a double arch newly opened in the wall to admit the sound of the organ placed in a chamber adjoining. Adjacent to which on the east is the vestry, also modern and containing a piscina.

The new font is of Perpendicular character and has a fine wood cover. The old font, which is Norman, having a circular bowl is in the churchyard. <The church is always open. The churchyard is beautiful and most carefully kept.> The general effect of the church is very good and the original features have evidently been carefully reproduced.

Puddlestone is another church which had been recently restored before Glynne's visit, and wins his approval for the interior 'being richly arranged for high ritual'. Some of the stained glass in one of the windows of the south aisle may be designed by Pugin – no wonder Glynne approved!

Aconbury [90/47] S. John 13 August, 1867

An interesting church, small but lofty, comprising merely a nave and undivided chancel with bell-cot over the west end. It was once connected with a religious house and there is perhaps on this account more of height and dignity than usual with small churches. The west end has a fair window, transitional from Early English to Decorated, having three tall lights (the central the highest) with trefoil heads and three quatrefoils above, the whole included under a pointed arch on clustered shafts having good cylindrical mouldings. On the north side are two windows of like character, but with two lights and one quatrefoil above. At the north-east and south-east are single lancets. Beneath the windows externally runs a string course, interrupted on the south by two doors now closed. <In the south wall near the west and high up is an arched door or opening.>

The roof is high-pitched and new – of coved form and panneled. The east window is of a common Herefordshire type, of three lights under a pointed arch unfoliated. There is a large piscina with trefoil head, set further west than usual in the south wall. There is ascent of one step marking the boundary of the chancel. The seats are all open and new – of pine – as also the pulpit. The whole is very carefully restored, and the windows have coloured glass. The font has an octagonal bowl. At the west end is a pretty original porch of wood with open framework and some good carving representing angel figures and strong braces.

Aconbury church is now closed.

Allensmore [90/46] S. Andrew 13 August, 1867

This church has nave and chancel without aisles, a western tower and south porch. The latter of wood and within it is a doorway with semicircular arch apparently Norman, the mouldings taking rather an unusual direction, as it were shouldered. The chancel arch is pointed and very plain, having continuous mouldings. There is a north door to the nave with continuous mouldings. On the south side of the nave is a fine and curious Edwardian window of three lights – each foliated and a large trefoil in the head which is double cusped. One window on the north is of two lights unfoliated, others are Perpendicular with flat arch and square head. The roofs have been renewed and are tiled. The tower is strongly built, has battlement and some buttresses – west is [a] window of two lights square-headed, belfry windows of two plain lights – and west door. The tower is probably Perpendicular. In the churchyard on the south is the shaft of a cross on steps. At the north-east a vestry has been added, and may possibly replace the original one.

Bishopstone [90/56] S. Laurence 15 August, 1867

A small church much modernized in a liberal and expensive manner, yet not wholly up to the mark of the present day. It is cruciform, without aisles, the transepts being shallow and as chapels – and no central tower or crossing. At the west end is a small bell-cot.

The west end has a two-light Decorated window, set between two small Norman windows and above these a modern circular window. The windows north and south of the nave are single lancets – those in the transepts are of the common Herefordshire type, of three lights. The chancel has a Decorated east window of three lights, and north and south of two lights. The arches opening to the transeptal chapels are pointed, on circular columns with octagonal caps. The roof appears to be new, that of the chancel is painted, with heraldic shields. There is a cinquefoil arch with piscina south of the altar. The interior has rather a sumptuous effect, but the woodwork is heavy – the open benches too high and intrusive, as also the seats for the choir. The chancel is laid with fine tiles. The font is poor. There is a large organ at the west end, rather too much for the church. The porch is of wood.

The restoration and ornamentation of the church was chiefly promoted by its rector, Archdeacon Price, circ. 1840.

The restoration here was early (1840), before the Ecclesiological movement had got fully into its stride, and this probably explains Glynne's rather guarded endorsement of the changes – 'not wholly up to the mark of the present day'. The organ was built by Father Smith for Eton College in 1700, and was transferred to Bishopstone in 1844. The 14th-century timbered south porch was transferred from the old church at Yazor (p.34).

Brinsop [90/55] S. George 15 August, 1867

A small church of some interest, and lately much restored. It has nave with north aisle, chancel and a shingled belfry over the west end, with tiled roof and containing three bells.

The nave and chancel are in one body, and the north aisle is equal to it in length; the arcade is of four pointed Early English arches on circular columns with octagonal capitals. The roof is of open timbers and has tie-beams. The aisle has a lean-to roof, its windows Decorated of two lights, some windows have no foliation. <One north window is of three lights which are trefoiled.> There is a rood screen between the nave and chancel. In the north wall is a good deal of rich Norman sculpture belonging to a doorway – the arch mouldings having angel figures within Norman arches and shafts on square bases. The tympanum has a figure of St. George and a rich border of angel figures and signs of the zodiac. <There are other scattered pieces of Norman ornamentation which appears to have been connected with doorways – and figures of serpents, etc.> The chancel has a Herefordshire east window of three lights unfoliated, and the central not arched. In it is some good ancient coloured glass in which appears the figure of a knight under an ogee canopy – several other canopies of fleur de lys. On the south of the chancel is a pointed recess with piscina and in the east wall two octagonal brackets with Tudor flower. The seats are open and of pine – the pulpit of oak. The font has a plain circular bowl on stem and square plinth. The south doorway has continuous mouldings and near it is a large stoup. There is a sepulchral slab with floriated cross. <In the parish of Brinsop is a remarkably fine specimen of an ancient mansion of the thirteenth century, moated and retaining much of its original features.>

The tympanum of St. George and the dragon and the voussoirs over the vestry door are now recognised as outstanding works of the Herefordshire School. The figure of the knight in the east window is also of St. George, patron saint of the church, and is an example of excellent stained glass of the 14th century.

116

Hereford All Saints [96/39]
[Undated, but placed between other entries for 1867]

A respectable parish church consisting of a nave and chancel each with side aisles, the south aisle of the chancel extending wider than that of the nave, and a tower crowned with very lofty stone spire at the west end of the north aisle. <This is of a type really belonging to Herefordshire. There is no chancel arch and the roofs are high.> There is no clerestory and the exterior as often in this county is irregular – but there are good portions of each of the three pointed styles. The tower is plain and embattled – the spire ribbed, very large and lofty: considerably surmounting the cathedral in the views of the town; at its base are small canopied windows.

The chancel has a south porch opening on the street, Perpendicular work and very elegant. It is small and shallow, having flat embattled parapet and a flat stone groined roof – the outer arch is moulded, has fine double feathering and enriched spandrels. <The old pews and galleries were cleared away about 1857 – the state of the church much improved, though there are still pues with poppy-ends doors but on a regular plan [*sketch*]. The organ has been removed to the south aisle.> The tower occupies the space of two arches at the west end of the north aisle and the north aisle is larger and wider than the south. <This church is not unlike that of Weobly in its general character and features.> The nave is divided from the south aisle by five Early English arches upon massive circular columns, the eastern arch being very narrow and the respond a foliated bracket. On the north are only three arches beyond the steeple. <The clerestory windows are closed. The south piers have octagonal capitals.> The windows on the south of the nave are square-headed, having good Decorated tracery of three lights. Those on the north seem to be mutilated having three plain lights. A similar one at the west end is of five lights. <The windows south of the chancel are of two lights and Decorated, in the nave square-headed and Decorated of good local type.> <There is an arch between the south aisle of the nave and that of the chancel, part of which is made into a vestry. There is a south porch to the nave as well as to the chancel, of somewhat similar character.> The roof of the nave is a fine open one, with open panning above the beams and wooden figures – that of the north aisle is of later date, more of a domestic character resembling Eltham Palace, and very good of its kind. The chancel is divided from its aisles by high pointed arches – its south aisle extends a little beyond that of the nave and has Decorated windows of two lights; also some stone corbels of Early English appearance beneath its coved roof. The church has also a coved roof panneled. On each side of the chancel are five rich wood stalls having ogee canopies feathered and elegant tabernacle work surmounted by a cornice of Tudor flower. There are also some carved wooden seats. <The north chapel of the chancel has three-light windows of the plain Herefordshire kind – three lights without foils – the central not arched. In this chapel there is a fine Decorated piscine, with rich foliation and ball-flower on the mouldings.> In the north aisle is a very fine geometrical Decorated east window of four lights, and also a rich niche with water drain, three foil feathering and ball-flower in the mouldings. At the west end is a large organ.

Burghill church

Burghill [90/57] S. Mary 15 August, 1867

This church is a fair specimen of the Herefordshire large village church – has a clerestoried nave with aisles, chancel, south porch and western tower. The roofs as usual of good slope and tiled, without parapet. The nave is wide and lofty and the prevailing features are Early English, with some plain Edwardian. The arcades of the nave are Early English and each has five pointed arches – the northern pillars being circular with moulded capitals – the southern octagonal with circular capitals. The north-west respond seems to be Norman. The clerestory has no windows on the north, those on the south are irregular – one next the east is of two plain pointed lights – the others look as if they had been inserted in a debased period – one plain oblong single – one of three lights square-headed and unfoliated. At the west of the north aisle is a single lancet window – and there is one plain oblong single light in the same aisle and one closed at the west of the south aisle. The windows of the south aisle are bad modern Gothic, inserted probably when the tower was rebuilt: but in the north aisle is a window having two ogeed lights trefoiled. There is no chancel arch; but a curious rood-loft remains with its screen. The loft has good wood Perpendicular panneling and tracery, with some ornamented cornice and fringed arches. There is a piscina curiously placed above on level with the loft, on the south side, shewing that there was once an altar there. <This piscina has a bowl, with ogeed trefoiled niche.> The chancel is long, has on the north one small Norman window closed, at the south-east a window of two lights with lozenge above them. Another south aisle window is plain Edwardian of two lights. The east window is large, of three lights which are simply trefoiled. There is no piscina but some stone brackets against the east wall. On the north side is an original vestry. In the chancel is a Perpendicular alabaster tomb with effigies of a knight and lady, said to be Lord and Lady Milton – the tomb has panneling with niches and angels bearing shields. The knight has a camail [*a protective coat of mail*] of chain – the lady a kind of mitred head-dress, but somewhat mutilated.

The chancel is laid with new tiles. There are two organs (one not used of barrel sort) and two fonts. In the vestry is a curious leaden one of circular form and Norman character, having scrolled and arched moulding. The other, in use, has a cup-shaped bowl, which is modern – on a Norman base, ornamented with arches having images within them. The south porch has open work and a tiled roof. The tower built in 1810 is of poor modern Gothic. The churchyard is remarkably large and in it on the south side are high steps in front of the shaft of a cross.

The fonts described by Glynne appear since to have been combined – for the font at Burghill now consists of a leaden bowl, the upper part of which is original and decorated with an undulating leaf frieze; this now stands on the Norman stone stem carved with the figures of Christ and the twelve apostles enclosed within a Norman arcade. The effigies on the tomb-chest are those of Sir John and Lady Milbourne, c.1440.

119

Rowlstone [90/54] St. Peter 16 August, 1867

A very interesting church in a secluded and highly picturesque district – consisting of nave and chancel only, and west tower and large south porch. There is much of Norman work and the church has been recently restored. The south doorway and chancel arch are fine Norman, and the walls of nave and chancel seem to be mainly of that period – all the windows being original except one inserted Perpendicular one of three lights on the south side. The east window of the chancel is also Perpendicular of three lights, but the north and south windows single and narrow Norman ones.

The south doorway has two orders of arch mouldings, one [*text unclear*] on has the cylinder. There is one order of shafts with sculptured capitals representing animals etc. In the tympanum is a vesica in which is Our Lord seated in glory surrounded by four angels.

The chancel arch has one order of shafts with sculptured shafts and abaci – the figures being varied. One order of moulding is cylindrical and has sculptured imposts which is returned by the wall. The hood has a course of moulding with hollow squares. There are also figures flanking the capitals on the north side.

The tower arch is a flattish one springing at once from the wall. The chancel has a new coved and ribbed roof and the sacrarium laid with new tiles. Against the east wall are stone brackets – and there is at the east end some curious ancient iron-work with fleur de lys pattern which seem to have formed candelabra. It is attached to the wall and draws out. There is a new pulpit of stone. The font has a circular bowl, on a cylinder. The tower is low and massive, divided by one string-course and without buttresses. A west window of plate tracery has been added – two lancets with cinquefoiled circle above – the other openings are mere slits. The roof is partly of wood and capped by a pointed finishing of tiles.

The material is redstone. In the churchyard is the base of a cross on high steps.

The tympanum representing Christ in Glory is the work of the Herefordshire School; the capitals of the chancel arch are also richly carved with human figures (one of which is inverted and may represent St. Peter), angels and various birds. The pair of 15th-century wrought-iron bracket candelabra are, I believe, unique.

Kenderchurch [96/40] S. Mary 16 August, 1867

A small church, in bad condition, situated on a lofty eminence apart from houses. It has only a nave and chancel with the outer walls whitewashed, south porch, and low turret at the west end. The windows on the south are all mutilated and on the north of the chancel are none. The east window is Perpendicular, of three lights. Over the south doorway is seen some of the sculpture of a Norman tympanum. Near the south doorway is a stoup. The chancel arch is rude and obtuse, and the chancel has the original coved roof with ribs forming pannels.

The most remarkable feature is the rood screen and loft which are in a pretty complete state. Under the loft is a panneled roof with ribs and bosses, and there is a kind of fringed cornice above. The screen has rather plain work with mullions and but little tracery, and beneath the cornice facing west are brackets or spandrels. On the south side of the rood-loft is an arched doorway which must have led to the rood-stairs. In the east wall appears as usual a stone bracket. At the north-east corner of the chancel is a square aumbrye. The font is circular and of cup-shape. The roofs are covered with flags. The belfry is of wood.

Four years after Glynne's visit, there was a drastic restoration: the sculpture of the Norman tympanum has vanished; the screen survives, but not the loft – it is mostly Victorian, but incorporates late medieval work.

Killpeck [90/53] S. David 16 August, 1867

This small church is well known as a highly enriched specimen of late Norman work and has been well illustrated by G. R. Lewis. It has been restored and is now in very good condition. The plan consists of nave and a chancel of two divisions, the eastern being apsidal, of semicircular form, and vaulted. A new bell-cot is erected over the west end. The exterior has a remarkable corbel-table under a moulded tablet, with a variety of heads and emblematical figures. <In the south doorway are figures set adjacent to the capitals of the shafts, of symbolical nature.> The windows are single with semicircular heads having shafts and ornamental mouldings. At the west end are three projecting figures externally. The buttresses are flat-faced. The south doorway has some splendid sculpture, and figures in the tympanum and shafts with animal figures in the capitals. One window on the north has a trefoil head. The arches from the nave to the chancel and from the chancel to the apse are both highly ornamental. The chancel has lancet windows with trefoil heads. The apse is vaulted and ribbed, the ribs having chevron ornament and carried on shafts. The windows of the apse are round-headed. The font is early – a very large circular bowl (of marble) on central stem and four cylindrical shafts with caps of foliage. The bell-cot over the west end is new and has two enriched arches of Norman character for the bells.

The excellence of the Romanesque carving at Kilpeck was already recognised in Victorian times; G.R. Lewis had depicted the sculpture in his Illustrations of Kilpeck Church, Herefordshire *in 1842.*

122

Madley [96/17] S. Mary [Undated, but ? August 1867]

This is a spacious and very interesting church, rich in fine specimens of both Early English and Curvilinear work – and comprising a nave with two aisles on the south side and one on the north, a tower at the west end, and a very fine chancel with a multiangular east end, and rendered more curious by a large crypt beneath it. There is a north porch to the nave, which has a Norman window. The tower, the principal part of the north aisle and the piers and arches of the nave are Early English – the additional south aisle, the chancel and many windows are Curvilinear of the finest character. The tower has a small aisle or chapel on both north and south sides with lancet windows and opening to it by pointed arches – the buttresses of the tower are flat – the lower part on the west side has a moulded doorway with shafts, surmounted by a label. Above this are three lancet windows with mouldings and clustered shafts – the next stage has on the west two lancets, on the north and south a plain two-light window, the belfry windows have each three equal lancets, and the parapet is of later date, embattled. The aisles against the tower have a lower roof than the other parts. The interior is spacious and beautiful – the nave has on each side a row of six fine Early English arches with circular pillars having octagonal capitals – over the piers on the south are small lancet windows opening to the aisle. An additional row of arches divides the south aisle from the chapel which has been added on that side – these arches together with the chapel are of Curvilinear character, five in number, with light piers of lozenge form having four shafts attached with ball-flower in the capitals. This chapel does not extend quite to the west end – its south windows are of three lights – and that at the east end a very beautiful one of five lights entirely filled with ancient glass of most brilliant colours. The east and west gables of this chapel are crowned with ornamental crosses. The chancel has a roof of high pitch, beneath which runs a cornice of ball-flowers. The side windows are some of two, some of three lights – at the east end which forms three sides of a hexagon are three windows – the centre one of three lights containing some rich stained glass. At the angles of the east end are set buttresses, surmounted by square pinnacles set lozengewise, and having ball-flowers in hollows in the angles. There are also square pinnacles flanking the west side of the chancel near where it meets the nave, with shafts set in hollows at the angles. Between the nave and chancel is a wood screen apparently of Curvilinear period, and on each side of the chancel arch are small arches <hagioscopes> in the corners opening to each of the side aisles. There are carved stalls in the chancel, and at the east end of the north aisle a fine ancient pue with covering over it and screen of Rectilinear work. On the south side of the altar are three equal stalls trefoiled, and having the ball-flower in their arch mouldings, and springing from clustered shafts there is a fourth containing a piscina. There is a square cupboard under a window on the north side and an altar tomb with two figures to Richard Watson of Sugwas 1574. The crypt under the chancel is lighted by several trefoiled lancet windows – it has a groined ceiling of stone, the ribs springing from an octagonal pillar in the centre.

The font is of very large size, of black marble, the basin cylindrical, supported upon a massive shaft of the same form.

Sutton St. Michael [90/50] 17 August, 1867

A small church, now undergoing restoration – has only chancel and nave, with bell-cot over the west end. There is also a west porch which seems original and no other doorway. On the north of the nave is one small Norman window closed. Some other windows are of two lights with trefoil heads: but the chancel has a single Norman window at the east end and on the north.

The chancel arch is Norman – semicircular, but has a keystone and may have been altered. Under the imposts are [*text unclear*] mouldings. There are new seats, open with poppy-ends too high. The roof is newly tiled.

Sutton St. Nicholas [90/51] 17 August, 1867

This church has nave, chancel, south transept and west tower. The transept is rather of the nature of a short aisle and opens to the nave by two rather acute arches on an octagonal pillar. The nave has a single lancet on the north and one on the south set eastward of the chapel, on the north a Decorated window of four lights. The south chantry has at the end two lancet windows trefoiled and above them an Early English string. In the chapel is a stone bracket on the south wall and a piscina under a trefoiled arch. The roof of the nave is open timber-work – not bad – with tie-beams and spandrels and cusped openings above. The chancel arch is a plain pointed, on imposts. The tower arch a plain pointed one. There is a Perpendicular rood-screen and near it south-east of the nave a piscina enriched with ball-flower marking the place of an altar. The chancel is Early English – has on the south two lancets with trefoil heads and a priest's door. On the north is a lancet much splayed. At the south-east the window has in the eastern jamb a piscina with ball-flower ornament and trefoil head: and the centre of the cill has been oddly cut through. The east window has two lancets with trefoil heads.

The tower is Early English, without buttresses, has single lancets in the belfry and another single lancet in the west.

The seats are open.

In the churchyard is the original Norman font, of circular form.

West Hide [90/52] S. - 17 August, 1867

An interesting church, having nave with lofty wide south aisle, chancel, west tower and south porch. The church is in good order, recently restored.. There is as usual much of early geometrical work. The aisle is separated from the nave by two pointed arches upon an octagonal pillar with circular responds. The nave and aisle are short, but lofty and nearly of equal width. In the aisle the windows are of two lights and in the nave very similar. There is a new stone pulpit and a vestry has been added on the north in the form of a transept. In the south aisle is a sepulchral arch in the wall with plain moulding, under which are the figures of a man and woman. <The man is a civilian.> The tower arch is pointed and very low, of two orders on octagonal shafts with semi-Norman foliage in the capitals. The chancel arch is pointed on octagonal shafts.

The chancel has trefoiled lancets – at the north-east a two-light window verging to Decorated. The east window of three lights, Geometrical and early. In the east wall is an aumbrye – and each side of the east window brackets with mitred and crowned heads. On the south a trefoil-headed niche with a piscina. The chancel is stalled, laid with tiles and on the altar are candlesticks. The font has a circular bowl on a stem. The porch is new, the doorway within it has continuous arch mouldings and a stoup in the east jamb.

The tower is very low but massive and has a tiled pointed roof and no buttresses. On the west side a single lancet – and lancets in the belfry – and some slit-like openings irregularly set

Weston Beggard [90/50] All Saints 17 August, 1867

This church has a nave and chancel without aisles, west tower and south porch. The chancel arch is Early English, pointed, upon corbeled shafts. The chancel has on the north one single lancet with trefoil head and one double. <The shafts have good capitals.> The east window is modernised, as are most of the other windows throughout the church, save some on the north of the nave. The tower arch has good deep mouldings. The chancel has on each side a fine Decorated sepulchral arch in the wall. That on the south has rich double feathering with foliage in the spandrels and the canopy of ogee form with finial and flanking pinnacles. That on the north has the ball-flower in the mouldings. The south doorway has rather an obtuse arch with canopy of ogee form with finial and flanking pinnacles. That on the north has the ball-flower in the mouldings. The south doorway has rather an obtuse arch with continuous mouldings. The tower is Perpendicular, strongly built with corner buttresses and no string; has base mouldings, parapet and gargoyles. The west window of two lights, as also those of the belfry.

Withington [90/49] S. Peter 17 August, 1867

This church has a nave and chancel only, with a south porch and western tower with stone spire. The chancel is undivided from the nave except by a wood screen of Perpendicular character mounted on a stone base and having tracery and panneled spandrels. In the nave are some square-headed windows, some Perpendicular, some Decorated, and of two lights; on the south is one with two trefoil heads and on the north one single lancet. <One window on the south of the nave is of late character, square-headed and transomed, of three lights.>

The chancel has two lancets on the south, one on the north, the south-western having a trefoil head. The east window Perpendicular of three lights. Under the south-east window is a trefoil-headed piscina and to the west of it another set lower in the wall without foliation. <There is a vestry north-east of the nave.> The nave has a new open roof, coved and ribbed. The tower arch is pointed, with bold continuous mouldings. The interior is in very good condition – with new open seats – but the walls lean outwards. The font is a new one with marble columns and of Decorated character. The chancel is fitted with stalls. The porch a new one of wood.

The steeple is a fair composition: the tower of good masonry, has moulding round the summit, corner buttresses and no string course, very good base mouldings and a turret at the south-east. On the west side is one slit-like opening – also a wide lancet – and a trefoil-headed lancet on the north and south, no belfry windows, nor west door. The spire octagonal, has at its base trefoil-headed lights set on the alternate sides.

There is an ancient lych-gate.

Ocle Pichard [90/28] S. James 17 August, 1867

This church has an odd exterior – a long narrow nave and chancel with south porch – and a singular-looking western steeple of which the two lower stages are of stone, of very small dimensions, and crowned by an upper story of wood, which overhangs and looks top-heavy, having a pointed roof. The lower parts have slit openings and no buttress – and very little character, save a large west doorway. The tower arch to the nave is pointed and very narrow. The roof is new. The architectural features are but poor. The windows have mostly two trefoil-headed lights under a pointed arch, but some are single – that at the north-west of the chancel has the rear arch ogeed. The east window is Perpendicular of three lights. On the north of the chancel is an ancient vestry with square-headed windows. In the south-east window-cill is sunk a round piscina. The priest's door is pointed with ogee arch internally. The chancel arch is pointed and very rude, without moulding or impost. The font has a plain octagonal bowl, on square plinth. The south doorway has continuous arch mouldings. The church is pewed.

The tower has now lost its upper storey of wood, and is surmounted by a copper-covered broach spire.

Hope Mansell [90/62] S. Andrew June 12ᵗʰ, 1868

A small church in a rural picturesque village, consisting merely of nave and chancel, with south porch and a shingled bell-cot over the west end. The nave is whitewashed and not improved – the chancel has been restored and partly rebuilt – with new roof and ridge-crest – and a better stone-laid base within. The chancel is Early English originally. On the south of it are two lancets, one of which has a trefoil head. The east window is of three lights, quite plain and unfoliated. On the south is an octagonal piscina beneath a trifoliated niche. The chancel arch is not in the centre, pointed with strong mouldings springing from the wall. The windows of the nave are bad modern insertions, save one lancet at the south-east. The old font, with a cylindrical bowl, is in the churchyard and an ugly modern one in use.

Ashperton [89/4] S. Bartholomew 10 June, 1869

This church has nave and chancel, without aisles, but north and south transepts, and a western tower which is modern and ugly. There is also a large south porch. The arches opening to the transept are plain pointed, also that to the chancel. The east window is of true Herefordshire type – of three plain lights of which the central one is not arched. The other windows are mostly of two lights, each trefoiled.

Munsley [89/3] S. Bartholomew 10 June, 1869

A small church having only chancel and nave – with wooden bellcot over the west end. The chancel arch is Norman – small and plain – the windows single lancets. The walls have been partially rebuilt.

There is herringbone masonry in the east wall.

Pixley [89/3] S. Andrew 10 June, 1869

A small church in a very secluded situation, lately put into excellent condition. The walls have been in some measure rebuilt. There is only a nave and chancel with a wooden belfry over the west end. There is no chancel arch but a new screen dividing the chancel. The windows are mostly single lancets.

Glynne's 'new screen' is hard to understand: the Royal Commission on Historical Monuments attributed the screen to the 14th century, with later additions; Pevsner doubted whether it was early. The screen is certainly attractive, rude and rustic: dendrochronology could settle the issue.

Winforton [90/63] S. Mary 11 June, 1869

This is a church of more interest [*i.e. than Willersley*] – has a wide single nave and chancel, with a north transeptal chapel and south porch and a western tower. The latter is of stone in its lower part, without buttress and with two tiers of small slit openings – the upper part is of wood frame-work, with tiled pointed roof, and slits opening to the belfry. On the whole, the effect is picturesque. The tower has a pointed doorway opening to the nave. The nave has one very small single lancet on the north, but no other window on that side. On the south are some double lancet windows of this kind [*sketch*]. There is no chancel arch, but the transept opens to the nave by a pointed arch on octagonal pillars. The transept has a three-light window of the Herefordshire kind of three lights, the centre not arched. The chancel has a similar window at the east, and on the south a priest's door and a two-light window with trefoil heads. On the south is a plain piscina. The roof is coved, but tampered with and the chancel portion has a wood cornice. Externally the roofs are tiled. The porch is of wood, open frame-work. The font has a plain octagonal bowl. The church is pewed in ugly fashion. In the churchyard are some fine yews and the situation is very pretty.

There was extensive restoration of the church in 1895.

Willersley [90/62] S. Mary 12 June, 1869

A very mean and small church, scarcely deserving of notice. It is a single oblong building without distinction of chancel – has a south porch and wooden belfry. The porch also of wood. It is possible that the walls may be ancient, but they are covered with stucco and all the windows are modern. On the north side there are no windows. The only ancient feature is the south doorway, which has indications of Norman work in the ornamentation of the flat lintel where is a course of hollow squares and star ornament. The arch if it ever existed is hidden by the porch. The font modern and the church is pewed.

The lintel (dated to 1100 – 15) is similar to those in the nearby churches of Bredwardine (q.v.) and Letton. Willersley church is now a private residence.

Kinnersley [89/1] S. James August 1869

This church has nave with aisles, chancel and tower at the west end of the north aisle and a south porch. The tower is massive and a fair specimen of the rather uncommon saddleback form – in the upper part on the east and west running into gables, and the roof of tiles sloping like a saddle on the north and south. The tower has no buttresses but one string course just at the base. The openings are small and narrow, single, and some with trefoil heads. <The tower opens to the nave by a pointed doorway.> The west end of the nave has a side gable, the roof carried over the south aisle. The west window is a curious one with tracery of three lights rather transitional from Decorated to Perpendicular and inserted in an earlier wall which has a horizontal string with cable moulding and below is a door trans[itional] from Norman to Early English of uncommon form, having a narrow semicircular arch contained under a larger one and having shafts with odd capitals. <The north chapel or transept is closed.>

The tower extends northwards beyond the width of the aisle. The nave is wide – its arcades are not similar: the northern has four pointed arches on octagonal pillars with capitals – the southern has four pointed arches of Perpendicular character, having each four shafts set at the angles and hollow mouldings between – the shafts have capitals and stilted bases. Over the northern arcade appears an earlier string course. The north aisle towards the east expands into a sort of transept. The roofs are new and the whole interior has lately been renovated and put into a very good condition – the seats all open. The windows on the north are square-headed and of

Edwardian character – of three lights. At its east end is one of three trefoil-headed lights, under a pointed arch. The south aisle windows are also square-headed, of two and three lights and transitional from Decorated to Perpendicular.

The chancel arch seems to be a new one of Early English character on corbeled shafts with rich capitals of foliage and abaci. Over the chancel arch are octofoiled circles letting in light. There is a low stone screen dividing off the chancel and at the south-east the rood stairs. The chancel has good windows: just emerging from Early English of two lights and one single lancet at the south-west. The east window of the former kind, of three lights. These have new coloured glass. On the north and south of the altar is a trefoil arch going through the wall seen both externally and internally, also a piscina. On the altar are candlesticks. The porch and font are modern.

Eaton Bishop [89/9] S. Michael 13 June, 1870

An interesting church of the local type, having a clerestoried nave with north and south aisles, chancel, south porch and west tower. The prevailing features are Early English, but the tower is Norman, plain and early. It is of massive proportions, without buttresses and has two string courses dividing the stages. In the centre of the north side is a single rude window with semicircular head – and on the south are two set low down. The belfry windows are of two round-headed lights with central shaft. The tower is crowned by a shingled pointed roof. The tower arch to the nave is early Norman with edged orders and impost mouldings. At the west end of the north aisle is a single lancet. The other windows of the aisles are single lancets, except those at the north-eastern bay on each side which are raised and gabled, the northern of three lights [a] simply trefoiled oculus [*a round window or tracery light*] – the southern Decorated of two lights. The nave has Early English arcades, each of five pointed arches – the pillars being circular with octagonal capitals – those next the east [have] foliated capital[s]. The chancel arch is of similar character – above it is a large window of five arched lights which are trefoiled. The clerestory of the nave is a good specimen of unaltered Early English, with single lancet windows. The roof of the nave is high and slated. Near the east end of the north aisle is an ogee arch in the wall. In the south aisle is a cinquefoiled arched piscina. The chancel has on each side two good Decorated windows of two lights, with spherical trefoils in the heads. The east window is of five lights simply trefoiled, probably of Edwardian character and containing some ancient coloured glass. On the south side of the chancel are three sedilia of equal height, with ogee heads trefoiled and a piscina of similar figure. The roofs are open. The font has an octagonal bowl with flowered border and fluting.

The 'ancient coloured glass' in the east window is now recognised to be of outstanding quality, the finest in Herefordshire, from the same workshop which provided glass for Tewkesbury, Ludlow and Bristol in the early 14th century.

Preston on Wye [89/7] S. Laurence 13 June, 1870

The church has nave, chancel, chapel on the north of the nave, west tower and south porch – all in a neglected and dirty state. The chancel has on the north one lancet and one wider single window with trefoil head. On the south is an odd priest's door, the arch of which is curiously cusped or foliated. < [*diagram*]> To the east of this door is a two-light Decorated window, to the west a two-light square-headed Perpendicular one. The east window is of the common Herefordshire sort of three lights under a pointed arch, the centre not arched. The chancel is long – and there is no chancel arch – on the north of the nave is one plain small Norman window – on the south is a single lancet, and one of two plain unfoliated lights.

The transeptal chapel opens to the nave by a pointed arch. On its east side is a square light Perpendicular window of two lights; at its north end a Decorated window of two lights. Within the south porch is a Norman doorway – the arch of two orders – the outer has chevron ornament – and [?] capitals of shafts which have perished. The inner member is continuous. The porch is of wood – open framework with tiled roof. The tower is transitional from Decorated to Perpendicular, has corner buttresses and battlement – belfry windows of two lights – on the north-east a stair turret – on the west [a] good two-light window of late flowing character. There is no west door. The tower arch is pointed and continuous. The font has a circular bowl on a cylindrical shaft. There are some old open seats.

The church was restored by T. Nicholson in 1883, retaining the Norman doorways, the tower and the north transeptal chapel.

Blakemere [89/8] S. Leonard 13 June, 1870

This church has a nave and chancel, south porch and rude wooden belfry over the west end – the whole in a primitive state. The chancel arch is Early English – small and pointed, surrounded by much wall, having ribs in the soffit and springing from corbels with square abaci and a kind of engrailed capital. The chancel has at the east end three windows arranged thus: [*drawing*]. On the north is a single lancet – on the south is one single window with trefoil head and one square-headed Perpendicular of two lights. The south doorway is plain Norman – with semicircular head. On the south of the nave is one single lancet – at the west end a square-headed window of two lights, which looks Edwardian. The porch is of open wood framework.

The churchyard is large – in it is a fine shaft of a cross raised on many steps.

The church was largely rebuilt in 1877 by G. Truefitt, who made much use of the fabric of the preceding church. Most of Glynne's description tallies with the features seen today.

Bredwardine [89/11] S. Andrew 13 June, 1870

This church has nave and chancel without aisles, and a tower placed on the north side about the centre. The original work is Norman – on the north are two small windows of that date and one on the south. On both sides is a Norman doorway – that on the south a very good one, with square lintel and two orders of moulding which [are] cylindrical, the inner carried on shafts with cushion capitals, above which is a heavy impost moulding. The tympanum has in the centre a circle containing a wheel and square pannels. The north doorway is similar, but plainer, and has wheels in circles in the horizontal band above the lintel – the shafts are ornamented, one spiral, the other lozengy. At the west end of the nave is a Norman string course under the gable. On the south side of the nave is a three light Decorated window of rather odd tracery. There is no chancel arch. The chancel has no windows on the north. The east window is of three lights with trefoiled arches, and on the south is a similar two-light window. The tower abuts greatly on the nave – is plain and without buttresses – has plain battlement and one single narrow window but has very little architectural character.

The font is cup-shaped on a stem with shafts attached.

The carved lintels over the north and south doorways should be compared with those at nearby Letton and Willersley (p.136), and are probably by the same hand(s). In 1877, Robert Kilvert, the diarist, accepted the living at Bredwardine, and died two years later; he is buried in the churchyard.

Brobury [89/12] S. Mary 13 June, 1870

A small church with only chancel and nave, and porch and bellcot over the west end. There are single lancet windows on the north and south of the nave. The east window has two lancets set high in the wall – on the north-east of the chancel is a single wide lancet much splayed – at the south-east a window with two trefoil headed lights and a lozenge above them. On the south is a priest's door. In the north wall of the nave is a sepulchral arch. The porch is of wood with open panneling. The roof is of coarse woodwork. The bellcot has niches for two bells.

The church was later abandoned. The chancel alone remains, and is now connected to a private dwelling.

Middleton-on-the-Hill [89/14] S. Mary 30 September, 1870

A small church in a secluded spot shaded by large trees. It has only chancel and nave with a west tower. The walls are rather lofty and with high-pitched roofs, and seem to be of Norman work. On each side of both nave and chancel are flat buttresses at regular intervals. Some windows are small Norman ones – set high – one on the north of the nave is a single-light window cinquefoiled – on the south of the nave is one late and bad window. In the chancel is a single lancet on the south and a priest's door. The east window is a triplet, each light cinquefoiled. There are Norman doorways both north and south of the nave – that on the north is closed – has good mouldings with chevron and pellet ornaments and imposts with the hollow squares – the door is flanked by quasi-pilaster buttresses upon which are head corbels. The south doorway has also impost mouldings and chevron ornament with square lintel and tympanum above. The south porch is of wood, with open work of a late character. There are some bad windows inserted on the south of the nave. The chancel arch is Norman, of two orders with plain semicircular arch. The font has a circular bowl.

The tower is very massive and without buttresses – has not much architectural character, but there are two stages, the base spreading out. On the west side is a narrow single lancet. The belfry windows are double. The parapet and pinnacles seem to be of late and debased work.

Kimbolton [89/13] S. James 1 October, 1870

The church has nave with south transept, chancel, south porch and west tower with shingled spire. The nave has on the south a single lancet; on the north one lancet with trefoil head, also one square-headed window with mullions destroyed, but the corbels of the label remaining, and one bad modern window. On the same side is a pointed doorway closed. The roofs are high-pitched and tiled, but with modern ceiling. The porch is large, very plain and rough – within it is a good pointed doorway with hood moulding. The transept has at the south end two lancets slightly trefoiled, and over them in the gable a pretty Decorated window of two lights, not foliated, with trefoil above them under the containing arch, which has a hood moulding with head corbels. On the east side of the transept are two single lancets. The transept opens to the nave by an obtuse arch of rude character. The chancel has on both north and south sides an obtuse single lancet, and on the south a priest's door closed. The east window is an old single obtuse lancet. The tower is after the fashion of the neighbourhood very massive and low and without buttresses. It has some single lancets in different tiers, but much concealed by ivy of which there is a very large store on the south – on the same side a pointed doorway. It opens also to the nave by a low arch more like a doorway. The spire is shingled, of broach form and heavy – the tower rises but little above the roof of the nave. The north wall of the church is bounded by a lane. On the south is a large churchyard.

St. Margaret in Eckley [89/27] 5 June, 1872

A small church in [a] secluded spot, but upon an eminence and approached by very bad roads.

It has nave and chancel, south porch, and over the west end, a quasi-steeple, the lower part of stone, the upper part a belfry of wood and overhanging. On its west side is an oblong slit and it opens to the nave by a plain doorway. The porch is of wood and has feathering in the gable. There are two bad modern windows in the nave and a new one of Decorated character. The interior is in fine condition and has new open seats. The chancel arch is low and obtuse, upon plain imposts. Across it is a remarkable and well-preserved rood-loft and screen – the loft supported on two wooden detached pillars which are charged with canopied niches and have longitudinal bands of foliage. The sloping part under the loft has panneling with fine bosses, and there are two cornices of vineleaves and grapes – also a course of Tudor flowers, thus marking the date.

The nave has an open roof of timbers, with collars and embattled cornice. The chancel is ceiled – has a poor east window with [a] square head of two lights – on the south a two-light window, each trefoiled and without hood. The sacrarium is laid with new tiles.

On the east side of the chancel arch appears a rude staircase all inside the church to the rood door. The font has an octagonal bowl, on stem of like form, quite plain. In the south wall of the nave is a sepulchral arch.

The churchyard is remarkably large, but has few graves.

The rood-screen and loft at St. Margaret's is one of the wonders of Herefordshire. The church is always open.

Bacton [89/25] S. - 5 June, 1872

The church has nave and chancel undivided, with a western tower and south porch. The exterior walls mostly whitewashed, and the roof covered with tiles. The character is generally plain and rude. The windows square-headed of two and three lights, and not labeled, of Perpendicular character. The east window has a transom – has three wide lights in the lower part and five divisions above. The nave has only one window on the north. There is no chancel arch but an arched timber forms the boundary of the chancel. The roof is open and has an embattled cornice – partly enriched with angel figures. In the chancel is a piscina with octagonal bowl scalloped, under a pointed arch; also some ancient wood benches with good carving of poppy heads crocketed. There is indication of a rood turret on the north in a plain projection. The nave is pued and with gallery. The tower low and plain, with embattled parapet and no buttresses; has two-light belfry window and other openings simple and oblong. The south doorway has continuous rich mouldings. The priest's door has flat arch, with moulding. The font has a circular bowl on a circular stem. The tower opens to the nave by a pointed doorway.

In the chancel is a remarkable monument against the north wall. It is of rather elaborate and sumptuous character, and has a grand canopy in the style of the Elizabethan period <The canopy is supported by Corinthian columns>, and two female figures, one representing Queen Elizabeth, the other the lady commemorated – and the inscription is curious, commemorating Jhane Elys of Newe Court "Sworne of Queen Elizabeth's hiden[?] chamber allways Wyth maide Queene a maide did ende my lyff".

The monument is to Blanche Parry, maid of honour to Queen Elizabeth; Blanche is depicted kneeling before the queen.

Llancillo [89/28] S. Peter 5 June, 1872

It is impossible to conceive a church in a more secluded spot than this – so beautiful, yet so very difficult of access. It is in a retired vale, near the Monnow river, surrounded by hills and with scarcely any regular road to it. It is a rude and homely small edifice, having nave and chancel only, a south porch and a gabled belfry for two bells in open arches at the west end. On the north of the chancel is a plain round-headed window which looks Norman, much splayed, and having internally a kind of graduated cill. The east window has a single lancet, barely pointed, and a similar cill. <There is an oblong recess in the north wall of the chancel.> On the south is a debased window of two lights and a priest's door of wood and with Tudor arch. There is no chancel arch, but there is a horizontal timber across the entrance to the chancel, above which is plastering. The roof of the nave has been repaired – is open, with collar and longitudinal ribs, like that at St. Margaret [q.v.]. There are in the nave on the south square-headed windows, of three lights unfoliated – on the north, one later, the lights not being arched. The whole is dirty and dilapidated. The font has plain octagonal bowl, on chamfered stem. The south porch is large and plain – its doorway has a Tudor arch. The outer walls are whitewashed. At the west end is a raised platform.

Twenty years after Glynne's visit, Llancillo's state was desperate: the south wall fell in, the door left open, the walls became cracked and crumbling; sheep wandered in and out of the nave; the roof tiles were blown off, the oak panelling stolen. The church was successfully restored by the Reverend Robert Whinney, and the charming building survives to this day. It was regularly used for worship until 2001, when it closed following the outbreak of foot-and-mouth disease. It may still be visited.

Garway [89/29] S. Michael 6 June, 1872

A curious church, consisting of nave and chancel with south chapel, and a tower singularly placed to the north-west of the west front at an uncommon angle with it and connected with it by an original passage. The chancel arch is good Norman, of three orders much enriched, and having double chevron ornamentation, the soffit charged with a kind of billet ornament. The shafts have capitals with abaci. The nave has on the north one lancet closed, and one window of two lancets without hood, but a trefoil between the heads. There is also a closed door – the wall is low and the ground has [risen] nearly to a level with the cill of the window. The windows on the south of the nave are Perpendicular square-headed, of three trefoil lights. The west end has a three-light Perpendicular window and under it a doorway with pointed arch and hood. There is a projection for rood turret on the south near the east end of the nave. The chancel is long, has on the north two lancets, one of which has a trefoil head. At the east end is a two-light window with obtuse heads. The south chapel is a late Perpendicular addition, and has late square-headed windows on the south of two lights – at the east a three-light window. <The arcade to the south chapel is closed.>

The font has an octagonal bowl on a stem. The tower has no buttresses and a pointed roof. The lower part has single lancet openings, those of the belfry have two. It is divided by one string course – has a stair-turret projecting at the north-east, lighted by slits. An oblique passage connects the tower with the angle of the nave lighted by a kind of lancet [light].

Garway church was built in the late 12th century by the Knights Templar; the original nave was round, and was so constructed as to represent the Holy Sepulchre in Jerusalem. The nave was excavated in 1927, and the foundations are still exposed.

Acton Beauchamp [93/7] S. Giles 24 April, 1873

A small church, much modernised comprising only nave and chancel with low western tower. The latter is without buttresses or string-course and has some semblance of Early English character – a lancet window in the belfry, and a slated pointed roof. On the south side of the tower is some early sculpture built into the wall of a Norman character. The south doorway is Norman – the outer order carried on shafts with moulded abaci and sculptured capitals, the eastern having clustered heads.

The font has an octagonal bowl set on a shaft. The chancel arch is obtuse and of very poor character – probably modern and all the rest of the church appears modern, with bad windows – but there are no windows in the north of the chancel.

The site on a woody hill is very beautiful.

The tower is medieval, and the lintel set above the south doorway is a section of an Anglo-Saxon cross-shaft, probably dating from the 9th century. The rest of the church was rebuilt in a Georgian style in 1819.

Docklow [89/48] S. - 25 April, 1873

A small church nearly as mean as Wacton, and more modernised. It has nave and chancel only – at the west end a low tower with pointed roof of shingles. <Tower has no buttress.> There is one small closed lancet in the chancel – the other windows are modern and wretched. The roof is covered as at Wacton with stone flags – internally are tie-beams. The font has an octagonal bowl on stem with eight detached shafts and appears to be new. The porch is of wood and dilapidated. The exterior is so finely mantled with luxuriant ivy as to conceal its deformities. The churchyard, as usual, is very large, and has but few graves.

In 1880 the nave and chancel were substantially rebuilt.

Wacton [89/48] S. - 25 April, 1873

A small and very mean church, is a mere oblong with no distinction of chancel – but has a south porch of brick and a wooden belfry over the west end. The east window is a single lancet – there is a priest's door on the south. One window south of the chancel has been renovated – in the nave are some plain slit-like windows and one with trefoil head. <The roof covered with stone flags.> The font has an octagonal bowl.

The church is within a very large enclosure but without graves. The south doorway has semicircular arch and hood.

Only vestigial remains of the walls of this church survive.

Evesbatch [89/45] S. Andrew 26 April, 1873

A small and rather mean church, having only nave and chancel, south porch and dilapidated bellcot over the west end, carried on timbers set inside. The whole has a neglected look. The south doorway is plain pointed, but on the door is some old iron work. There is no chancel arch, but the division of the chancel is formed by wood posts. On the south of the nave is a two-light Decorated window with obtuse arch. The chancel seems to have been rebuilt and has a Perpendicular east window of three lights. There is only one window on the north – and that modern and bad. The roof of the nave has plain tie-beams. There are a few old open seats. The font is a plain cylinder, of early character. The walls are of very rough masonry, covered with stucco.

Four years after Glynne's visit the church was substantially rebuilt.

Stanford Bishop [89/46] S. - 26 April, 1873

This church is in a lonely situation and has rather a look of neglect and decay. It consists of nave and chancel only, with western tower and south porch. The north and south doorways are Norman, the former plain, the latter has a cylinder moulding to the arch with shaft having abaci in the capitals. The inner member is without shaft, and in the door is some fine old iron work. The porch is much dilapidated and has the lateral windows with obtuse heads. The outer door has also an obtuse arch. There is one lancet on the north of the nave, and one obtuse-headed on the south: other windows of the nave are very bad. The tower arch to the nave is pointed upon imposts and very plain. There is no chancel arch. The chancel has been repaired and put into a better condition than the nave. It has windows of two lights under pointed heads – of which the eastern has trefoil foliation, the others have none. There is also an obtuse lancet at the south-west. There is on the south a piscina with semi-octagonal projecting beam under a trefoiled arch. Near it is a square recess. The roofs are open, rude and plain, with tie-beams. The font has a cup-shaped bowl on square base having pieces of foliage at the angles. There is a fine old chest formed of the trunk of one tree.

The walls of rough masonry, covered with plaster. The roof covered with tiles. The tower is very massive and low – scarcely rising above the roof of the nave – it is covered with a pointed tiled roof and has neither buttress nor string. On the south and west are rude single lancets, opening internally within a round arch. The belfry windows are merely rude slits.

The churchyard is remarkably large, but has few graves and those only on the south. West [?] are some very fine yew trees.

The church is no longer neglected nor decayed.

Stretton Grandison [89/41] S. Laurence 26 April, 1873

A small church, of pleasing character and in good order – has only nave and chancel, with western tower and spire, mostly of Decorated character. The nave has three windows of this kind on each side, all good of two lights. The chancel arch is pointed, springing from the wall without imposts. The chancel has a good east window of three lights. At the south-west is a square-headed window of two ogee lights, shouldered vertically. At the south-east is one somewhat similar, of one light only, the cill prolonged so as to form a sedile. Connected with it is a small trefoil piscina – opposite to it a square recess in the north wall, on which side the chancel has no windows. The sacrarium is laid with new tiles and the east wall has been coloured. The chancel has a boarded roof, that of the nave open and apparently renovated. The nave has open seats, with some good Perpendicular wood carving. The tower arch is pointed, springing from the wall without imposts, and the tower is open to the upper floor. The font is Perpendicular – an octagonal bowl panneled with quatrefoils and with figures of angels and emblems in zinc. The tower is narrow and without string course, has battlement and gargoyles and corner buttresses. <Six bells.> The spire is of stone, octagonal and ribbed, of elegant proportion. The belfry windows single, with ogee heads – on the west [side] a two-light Decorated window – above is a single light. The chancel has on the north some different masonry and indications of earlier work – as flat buttresses. At the north-east of the nave is a slight projection with slit lights, connected with the rood loft. The south porch is plain.

Yarkhill [89/42] S. John 26 April, 1873

This church has been restored and in great measure rebuilt – consists of nave and chancel without aisles, and west tower, which is ancient. The rest of the walls have been mainly rebuilt. The tower in its lower portion may be early and opens to the nave by an Early English arch, with plain soffit, on imposts. There is a trefoil-headed lancet on the south side. On the west side, two single windows with trefoil heads and transoms under an ogee head. Beneath the belfry story is a corbel table, which seems to shew that the upper story is a later Perpendicular addition. It has a battlement and square-headed Perpendicular windows of two lights. The south doorway of the tower is late Norman – the inner member continuous, the outer on detached shafts having square abaci and sculptured capitals of foliage. The hood has nailhead ornament and good corbels. The chancel arch on Early English shafts with capitals of foliage seems to be new. The windows lately put in are transitional from Early English to Decorated. The chancel has boarded roof. The font is new, in a Romanesque style. Over the north doorway appears some Norman sculpture. The seats are all open and there is an organ in the chancel. <The old timbers are used in the roof of the new porch. Some part of the chancel walls seems ancient.>

Bishops Froome [89/43] S. Mary 26 April, 1873

This church has been enlarged and much renovated. It had originally a long and wide nave with chancel and a western tower – to which a new north aisle has been added, and a chapel north of the chancel. There are some original Norman portions in the chancel and in the doorways of the nave. The chancel has on the north two narrow Norman windows – at the east a Norman triplet erected about 1847. On the south are three Norman windows and part of an original horizontal band with grotesque animal figures. On the south side is a trefoil-headed piscina, and a small oblong aumbrye. The sacrarium is laid with new tiles. The chancel arch is low, of late Norman work, the inner member has plain soffit, the two outer orders having shafts – one moulding plain, one chevroned. <There is a piscina on the south of the chancel arch.> Across the screen is a plain wood screen. The south doorway of the nave is a fine Norman one, of three orders – the inner continuous and cylindrical – the other two orders have shafts with abaci and varied capitals – one order has a kind of indented ornament inclining to Early English. The south porch is new and its outer doorway is fine Norman, of three orders. The windows of the south aisle are all new and of Norman character. The roofs appear to be new and are open. The nave is very long, and the new north aisle is not carried to its western end. The arcade to the aisle (of course new) has four good pointed arches with chevron ornament of Early English character on the soffits – the piers are of two clustered marble shafts, having varied capitals of foliage. This aisle has a high-pitched separate roof – its west end has two high windows, with a circle in the centre above them. There is a sepulchral recess in the south wall of the nave having nailhead ornament in the arch – under it is a very large effigy of a knight with huge shield, the legs mutilated. The font has a circular cup-shaped bowl, on a cylinder. The tower arch is pointed – of three plain orders – two continuous, the inner on octagonal shafts. The wall of the tower is very thick. On the west side is a two-light Decorated window – and the belfry windows are of this character. The tower is plain, with embattled parapet and divided by one string.

Bishop's Frome church is an amalgam of Norman and neo-Norman styles: the chancel dates from 1847, the nave and north chapel from 1861. The architect was F.R. Kempson of Hereford. The 'grotesque animal figures' on the south wall of the chancel externally are probably related to the Herefordshire School of Sculpture (Leonard, 2000).

Bullingham [96/66] S. - 27 April, 1873

A small church two miles from Hereford, but difficult to find, consists of only nave and chancel without visible belfry. The west end has been modernised as well as some other parts and some windows, but some single lancets remain. The roof is covered with flags, and there is some slight difference between that of the nave and that of the chancel. There is the shaft of a cross in the churchyard, which is beautifully shaded with trees.

This church has now been abandoned, and only its lower walls survive. A new church (St. Peter, Bullinghope) was built nearby in 1889 by F.R. Kempson.

How Caple [89/51] S. Andrew 12 May, 1874

The church is in a beautiful situation on an eminence within a sloping churchyard commanding [a] lovely view of the Wye and surrounding woods. It consists of a nave and chancel, south transept, west tower and north and south porches. The tower has a fair outline, with battlement and pinnacles erected 1693. The arch opening into the nave has a keystone, as also the west door. <The north porch is of the same date as the tower and the public path is on the north.> The nave has good sand stone masonry – on the north are two-light windows – one Decorated and one Perpendicular. The west window of the tower is Decorated, probably re-inserted. The transept opens to the nave by an arch of quasi-classical character, as that of the tower. In the transept are Perpendicular windows of two and three lights – and one single light with ogee head within an oblong on the west. The chancel arch is pointed on shafts. In the chancel the windows are mostly Perpendicular, one square-headed near the west set up high – the eastern of three lights containing coloured glass. The south-west window of two lights seems to be Decorated. The font looks modern. The south porch has a door with continuous arch mouldings – within it the door has an obtuse arch. The roofs have stone tiles.

The chancel is indeed medieval, the rest of the church being rebuilt in 1693 – 95.

Eye [89/49] SS. Peter and Paul 21 May, 1874

A large and interesting church lately restored and in fine condition comprising clerestoried nave with aisles, chancel with north chapel, west tower and south porch. The church is mainly Early English with a few later features.

The arcades of the nave are good – each has four pointed arches, with chamfered orders, on circular pillars with moulded capitals and responds – one capital on the south being rather more highly worked than the others. <The pillars of the nave have circular moulded bases.> The clerestory has windows in shape of quatrefoil, within plain segmental arch. The roof of the nave is high-pitched, having tie-beams moulded and with foliage and open tracery above. <sketch> The aisles are low and narrow, having windows with square heads and of two lights transitional Decorated to Perpendicular – but at the west of each aisle is a single lancet. The tower arch to the nave is very fine Early English of three orders, which are square-edged, and shafts having foliage and square abaci. The outer member is stilted. The chancel arch is pointed, upon octagonal capitals. The north chapel is wider and rises higher than the north side of the nave and has separate roof. It opens to the chancel by two sharp straight-sided arches like some in Hereford Cathedral, upon a circular pier having a capital of foliage somewhat Corinthian. Between this chapel and the north aisle is a pointed arch on octagonal brackets set upon animal heads. <Above the pier

on the north of the chancel is a medallion, containing sculpture.> The chancel has an open roof – on the south side is one trefoil-headed lancet, and one single lancet surmounted by a semicircular arch, set on shafts with capitals of foliage and having a cylindrical moulding. This now opens into a newly-added sacristy on the south of the chancel. The east window of the chancel is of three lights, probably Decorated in period of a Herefordshire type, but not very common – the two side-lights having transoms. <*sketch*> There is on the south a priest's door with trefoil head and elegant mouldings. On the same side is a triangular small piscina with moulding. The chancel is laid with new tiles.

The north chapel has on the north some lancet windows, at the east a plain Herefordshire three-light window; there is also in the east wall a piscina with trefoil arch. In this chapel are two fine altar tombs of alabaster, but of rather debased character – one has the effigies of a knight and lady and on the sides shallow sculptured figures of parents and children kneeling.

The fittings of the church are all of oak – everything is handsomely done. The font has an octagonal bowl on a stem. The clerestory windows externally are set in squares. The north doorway is semi-Norman with cylindrical moulding and one order of shafts.

The tower appears to be wholly new – probably replacing one of debased character – in pretty good Early English style with flat buttresses, but with battlement and circular stair-turret at the south-west rising high.

The roofs of the church are tiled and without parapets.

This is the last church in Herefordshire visited by Sir Stephen Glynne. He died on June 17th, 1874.

Glossary

This glossary defines only those terms which are now obsolete or rarely used.

Benatura: a holy-water stoup.

Camail: a kind of protective coat of mail.

Curvilinear: in the Decorated style.

Debased: usually describing a Perpendicular style used in the 17th and 18th centuries.

Edwardian: dating from the reigns of Edward I, II and III (1272 – 1377).

Faldstool: a stool with folding legs.

Feathering, feathered: cusping, cusped.

First Pointed: the Early English style.

Flamboyant: the last phase of French Gothic architecture, characterised by wavy or undulating window tracery.

Foliated: decorated with leaf forms; sometimes cusped; hence foliation: cusping.

Geometrical: tracery consisting of circles or foiled leaf-shaped circles, seen during the Decorated period.

Hood: hoodmould.

Lanthorn: an obsolete spelling of lantern.

Lychnoscope: a low-side window.

Middle Pointed: the Decorated style.

Miseries, miserieux: misericords.

Oculus: a round or oval window.

Panneling: rectangular compartments; hence panneled.

Rectilinear: the Perpendicular style.

Rood-turret: a stone turret built to house a staircase giving access to the rood-loft.

Sacrarium: the sanctuary.

Sepulchral arch: an arch over a tomb-recess.

String: a string-course.

Subarcuated: used of an arch with subdivisions formed by smaller arches.

Third Pointed: the Perpendicular style.

Toothed: having dogtooth ornament.

Triplet: a group of three lancets.

Tudor flower: the five-lobed Tudor rose, combining the red and white rose badges of the houses of York and Lancaster.

Vesica piscis: an almond-shaped halo, consisting of two arcs enclosing a figure of Christ or the Virgin.

Bibliography

Annett, D.M. 1999 *Saints in Herefordshire,* Logaston Press, Herefordshire
    2003 *Churches of the Bromyard Rural Deanery*, The Bromyard & District Local History Society

Boase, T.S.R. 1953 *English Art 1100–1216*, Clarendon Press, Oxford

Butler, L.A.S. *The Yorkshire Notes of Sir Stephen Glynne,* Yorkshire Archaeological Society, Record series (forthcoming)

Cox, D. (ed.) 1997 *Sir Stephen Glynne's Church Notes for Shropshire*, The University of Keele, Staffordshire

Cranage, D.H.S. 1884–1912 *An Architectural Account of the Churches of Shropshire,* Wellington, Shropshire

Jenkins, R. 1995 *Gladstone,* Macmillan, London

Keyser, C.E. 1904 *A List of Norman Tympana and Lintels*, Elliot Stock, London

Leonard, J. 2000 *Churches of Herefordshire and their Treasures*, Logaston Press, Herefordshire

Marshall, G. 1949–51 'Fonts in Herefordshire', *Transactions of the Woolhope Naturalists' Field Club*

Pevsner, N. 1963 *Herefordshire* in *The Buildings of England* series, Penguin, Harmondsworth

Phillott, H.W. 1888 *Diocesan Histories: Hereford,* S.P.C.K., London

Royal Commission on Historical Monuments, *Herefordshire Vol II East* 1932

Veysey, A.G. 1981 'Sir Stephen Glynne, 1807–74', *J. Flintshire Historical Soc.*, xxx. 151–170

Index